Miles of Motherhood

Sheila Scott

SANDBAR NE INVESTMENTS, LLC

ISBN: 979-8-9936019-1-5

Contents

For David, Audrey, and Ethan. You are my world, my miracles and dreams come true. There isn't a mile I wouldn't run for you.

Introduction

The race is not always to the swift, but to those who keep on running.
– Author Unknown

"I'm thinking about running the Disney Marathon," my friend Ginny said. We sat with our legs submerged in the shallow pool at the splash park, attempting not to melt while our shrieking toddlers waded around us.

I reached up to lift the brim of my sun hat and turned from watching our preschoolers to look her in the eye with surprise. "No. Way."

Ginny and I met in the grocery store. We must have always been running out of milk at the same time, and one day she broke the ice with, "Excuse me, but where do you put all your groceries?" Audrey, then a little over two, sat in the child seat of the shopping cart, facing me. Ethan, just fresh out of the oven, snuggled in his infant carrier, which I laid across the width of the cart.

"Oh, it's easy," I said. "I fit them all underneath Ethan's seat and put the bigger things on the very bottom. Sometimes if I have a lot, I tuck things here in the car seat around Ethan's legs."

Introduction

I pointed to the Craisin pouch and lemons. An instant and eternal friendship was born right there at the fish counter. Soon, it was story time at the library, park days with picnic lunches, and countless play dates at each other's homes. Although running was one of our favorite topics to chat about while the kids snacked on Gerber Rice Puffs, I didn't realize she had her eye on a 26.2 until we were fishing fresh swim diapers out of our bags at the splash park.

As I coerced another coating of thick sunblock over Audrey's tiny arms, Ginny explained, "I've always wanted to run one, and if I don't do it this year, it might be a while if we have a second child."

I thought, *"No kidding. That's why I did it before my two showed up and confiscated all my freedom."*

With a glint in her eye, she then suggested, "You should do it too!"

"Ha! No, no, no, thank you very much. I ran my "bucket-list" marathon. I'm quite happy with my four milers and Denise Austin Videos." The math was simple—Audrey would be in kindergarten, and Ethan would be in half-day preschool three whole mornings a week in the coming fall. The possibilities for those sweet nine hours were unlimited. I could get a part-time job, or take a cake-decorating class, maybe take up oil painting or even...buy a new shirt from somewhere other than Target. I allowed myself to wonder if I was too old to audition for the Rockettes.

"Ginny, if your heart is in this, I think you should do it. I am glad I got it off my life list, but the training takes on a life of its own—you won't believe how much time you have to spend running. You'll live in your running clothes. You'll be sticky with Gatorade and embarrassed at parties, because no matter how many trips you make to the buffet, it's still not enough food to dump in your furnace."

But always the encourager, I soon launched into a monologue about how much fun the actual race is. Even though it's 26.2 miles, and sounds completely ridiculous, it's practically a party—the easy part compared to the training, the reward. Like when a stranger on an airplane compliments our well-behaved, little travelers. The strangers have no idea the training we had to enforce to earn those compliments.

Ginny would certainly treasure the experience, but in my case, I was finally getting comfortable. Why on earth would I detour from the straight-away to the finish line and purposely make myself *un*comfortable?

Because. Just as there is something irresistible about the smell of a newborn's head, the appeal of the smell of Icy Hot at a starting line at six in the morning is just as enticing. So, despite the lack of practicality, my love of running was reignited back to that of an awkward teen at a rainy cross-country meet, enjoying fresh-picked apples that one of the moms brought. I wanted back in the club. I wanted a goal of my very own, to feel the inner strength after a good fifteen-miler. To drip with sweat and have dirt and grass clippings stuck to the back of my calves. Ooh, I would need to go shopping for running shoes because there are too many miles on the old ones—I *love* running-shoe shopping.

As I released the white-knuckled grip on my free time, Ginny sensed the weakening of my spine, like the way a child sweetly—and confident in the outcome—asks for just *one* more popsicle. "I'll talk to David tonight," I said. "He's heard one too many horror stories about runners' hips needing replacement and wants me to be able to golf with him when we're retired." I knew full well at that moment what I was getting myself into.

"Mommieee!" Oh no. In a warrior dash, I ran through the eight-inch-deep water toward Ethan, because I heard "the cry."

"What happened, monkey?"

"I, I, I hit mine head," my three-year-old cried.

"Ouch, let's get some ice. It's okay, it's okay, you are definitely getting a big bump there, poor little guy. Audrey, follow me please. We have to go."

We packed up our raisin-fingered children and I agreed to call Ginny with an update on how Ethan was doing. After calling her later to let her know it was just a little bump, very small, and he was acting like his normal three-year-old self, it was twenty-four hours later that we booked our hotels at Disney, and I registered for my second marathon. This time, as a mother of two.

What I was about to learn over the next several hundred miles, was that running and mothering are both endurance sports, with many of the same requirements: Equal parts of love, commitment, and a conscious willingness to experience pain. Progress is tracked and strange things are ingested. Sometimes there are injuries, and both can bring great happiness or terrible distress. We always wish for just a little more time, and we measure our endurance by surviving four hours of crying, or eight miles in ninety degrees. Runners and moms have a superpower of mental toughness that helps us get in the zone and cover the long miles all the way to the post-race party.

Chapter 1
Which Came First, the Runner or the Mother?

"Where do you feel like going for dinner tonight?" asked David. "How about Mexican?"

"Oooh, perfect, I could totally go for one of those giant margaritas at Don Pablo's, mmm," I replied, taking my freedom to do whatever I wanted whenever I wanted, completely for granted.

"Great, I'll call Matt and see if he and his friends want to meet us. The Sabres are playing tonight, so they'll probably come out for a few beers."

We weren't even engaged at this time. Both of us were in our mid-twenties in the mid-nineties. We had been together for a few years, and as we were driving to dinner I said, "I am not in any way, shape, or form in a hurry to have kids, so don't freak out, but I've been thinking a lot and I don't think I'm the type that will be able to drop a baby off at daycare. I mean, if we have to, that's one thing. But I think I'd like our goal for me to be a stay-at-home mom."

I had a great job in an academic department at Buffalo State College and began looking into doctoral programs to eventually pursue a faculty role, so this was not a back-handed way of trying to get out of working. It was simply imagining an infant in my arms and the possibility of having to turn it over to someone else for eight or more hours a day. It made me cry just thinking about it. Yet there was so much I wanted to do before becoming saddled with a stroller, so even though I wasn't pining for a collection of tiny clothes and socks, I felt it was one of those conversations people are supposed to have before they waltz down the aisle.

"Well, I would agree with that," he said. "I see Rebecca crying at her desk every day because she so badly wants to be home with her new baby. I get it, I do. But if we need two incomes, we will have to figure it out together and make it work."

Misty eyed, I agreed. "Okay." I smiled because no matter what the future held for us, what I knew was that we were on the same team and would find a way to work out whatever our circumstances brought.

Seven years later, we would see how this would turn out, and one thing became clear immediately—even though I was a runner first, mothering would come before running for a while, and I would miss out on a *lot* of future margaritas.

I often wonder how women my age got into running, as I run along reading the pink and white mileage stickers on people's cars and laugh at the funny ones like, "will run for wine," "running is cheaper than therapy," and my personal favorite, "if found on road, please drag to finish line." A lot of these stickers surely belong to moms. Moms who grew up with running parents and spent their Saturday mornings at races, picking up aid-station cups instead of in their jammies watching TV. Moms who had a friend invite them to power-walk a few miles in the neighborhood, or moms who were the state track star back in their day. There are running moms who wanted to drop a few pounds for the wedding or lose the baby weight, and someone told them that running just melts away the pounds. I have in fact said those very words to my own friends.

I became a runner when I was in the sixth grade, completely unaware that the positive side effects of running would be transferred to other areas of my life for the next forty plus years. Noticing that I was often afraid of the ball, a PE teacher suggested I run a one-mile fun run with kids from several area elementary schools. I have no idea why I agreed, but being too young to be consumed by fear probably helped. With little or no training, I showed up. And out of sixty students, I came in ninth in under eight minutes. That was all it took. I lived for track and cross-country for the next six years. It was love at first stride.

Being on those teams gave me unique friendships, and my emotional connection to the sport grew stronger. Daily two-hour practices, plus weeknight and weekend meets, equaled a lot of time to bond with the other runners. While my non-running friends were meeting for milkshakes and study groups after school, I was with the teams until dusk, frolicking through wooded trails, or listening to the gravel of the track beneath our feet. We shared snacks and tubes of Icy Hot with one another, and hung signs on each other's lockers for encouragement on race days. One race in particular had me rely on a teammate for a very tangible kind of help.

"My shoe!" I yelled to the cold, wet, bundled parents on the side of the racecourse. They clapped their gloved hands together and encouraged, "You're doing great!"

I realized they couldn't hear me through the rain, wind, and their cozy hats. "My shoe! I lost my shoe!" I shouted as I ran forward but pointed back toward the muddy stretch from which I just staggered. The parents still did not understand, but I finally spotted a teammate who was not running in the meet that day due to an injury. "Cristina! My shoe is back there. I lost it in the mud."

She waved the okay sign to me, then cupped her hands around her mouth and yelled, "We'll find it, just keep going!"

So, under that gray, misty sky, I kept going. With a little less than a mile to the finish, a cold, floppy, mud-caked sock on one foot, and a shoe barely hanging onto the other because the shoes were a size and a half too big to begin with, I kept going and actually felt pretty cool. Kind of tough in a way, and this kind of confidence was new to me as a tenth grader. I liked it, and I liked that everyone told my lost shoe story and thought it was a riot.

With only one finger, Cristina handed my shoe to me, quite relieved to be done with that chore. And for the remainder of the shoe's life, it was several shades browner than the other one.

My kids love that story—it gives them a view of their muffin-baking mom that they don't always get to see underneath the piles of homework and room-cleaning requests. Plus, to a kid, imagining their mother losing a shoe in the mud gives them more material for lovingly teasing us.

The training runs with my high school cross-country team near Rochester, New York were where running became forever a part of my identity. We had fall seasons that looked like the campus pictures on college recruitment post-cards. Our coach and English teacher at our high school, Mr. Williams, always reminded us to "look at the foliage." Of course, everyone picked on his little mantra, but he was right. And living in Florida now, I pine for the crisp, golden fall days with just enough chill in the air to keep me comfortable. The long-sleeve shirt and shorts days are a runner's favorite.

Our school was near a quaint little cider mill, so we developed a little tradition of tucking a few dollars in our shoes to buy cider and donuts on the way back from a long run. The smell of cinnamon and crunching leaves surrounded us. The owners were kind and accustomed to our sweaty pack. It was a safe area with little traffic, a lot of which was from ducks. There was the first yellow duck-crossing sign I had ever seen, and it is part of the magical backdrop of memories when I recall the pain of our shin splints and blistered toes.

Our suburb was in a period of building new homes, and we couldn't resist venturing down just-paved roads with the smell of new lumber amid skeletons of soon-to-be homes. We took a run break and walked around inside of them, imagining how they would look when completed. Running wasn't simply about grueling track workouts or gut-busting long runs, it was about exploring our world and being part of our communities.

In addition to helping us develop a love of colorful foliage, Mr. Williams was also the race organizer of our town's annual 5K Turkey Trot, which of course the team was expected to run in each year, day off from school or not. We loved it, and the race of a few hundred has grown to well over four-thousand runners, led now by one of my former teammates. It's a town tradition, where my friends are likely now running with their own children. I hope they remember to pack money for the cider mill.

Mr. Williams treated us like his own family and had us over to his house for spaghetti dinners at his family's huge farm table. Everyone was dressed in turtlenecks and oversized sweatshirts, and our pile of running shoes crowded the entryway. The house was large and sort of rustic and sat on acres and acres of apple orchards. We ran through the muddy lanes of apple trees on cool fall days, with a perfume-like smell of macintosh that no candle company could ever replicate. If ever fall was contained in a place, this was it, and fall was meant for running.

Following the Turkey Trot, our team went to The Kinney Championship Cross-Country meet outside of New York City. We piled in a multi-row van and saw the skyline as we finished the ten-hour ride. One year, the course was nothing more than icy lanes, and we begged our spikes to claw into the ice and keep us from falling down and getting trampled by hundreds of other high school runners.

But the tougher the conditions, the better the story-telling later on. We just ran no matter what. Too hot? Get more water.

Too cold? Too bad, you'll warm up. We ran in all conditions, and I am grateful for that because I can still do it now. Weather has no impact on whether or not I'll run. Well, since becoming a Floridian, if we have a hurricane that might be a different story. Otherwise, I just dress accordingly and pack enough water, or money for extra water along my route.

Many of us went to running camp for a week each summer, before each fall cross-country season. If you have never been to running camp, the title says it all. We ran first thing in the morning, ate breakfast, had some kind of athletic activity or craft, and ran one or two more times during the day. It was a tranquil place in the mountains of Pennsylvania, with considerably well-equipped cabins and lots of shaded, hilly roads.

As the week progressed, the miles increased, and so did the number of ice-pack-covered shins. The last day always included our longest run, which was between seven and ten miles. And in the evening, we performed our end-of-the week, humorous skits on stage, poking innocent fun at our resident coaches in front of all the other campers.

Once back to our cabin, we spread out all our remaining snacks from home and pigged out. Of course, those snacks were largely granola bars and peanut butter crackers, rice cakes and GORP. It's funny how you remember the goofy things from trips like that, and the pain of the workouts is forgotten. The twisted ankles healed, the sunburns on our cheeks faded, but our quads, friendships, and love of running grew stronger.

We started our fall season as soon as we returned, and the twice-weekly meets began. For a long time, I never felt like a great runner. I wasn't very fast, I always felt a little heavier than the other girls, and even many of the rail-thin boys, but I did improve each year and even helped the team by placing ahead of similarly matched runners from the other teams. So even though I wasn't breaking state championship records, I was breaking my own records.

Achievement through running empowers teens as well as grown women who are out there running their very first laps around the neighborhood, or their very first races. They are proving to themselves that they are stronger and more capable than they ever thought possible.

Chapter 2
Runners, on Your Mark!

When I look back on the pre-kid days of our youth and early married life, it's like watching a movie of someone else's story. Even when doing something as simple as going out for dinner, I noticed the families with kids. Always with a stained diaper bag, and a slimy high chair whose perimeter was surrounded by partially gnawed french fries. I didn't quite understand the appeal. I was still able to enjoy conversation without interruptions, and read menu choices as though my life depended on it. When the waiter came by, frazzled and busy, we could sit there like kings and say, "No hurry, take your time." After all, we had worked a full 40-hour week for heaven's sake—we were exhausted!

Hilarious, we had *no* idea.

Following a typical night out at a chain restaurant or local wing place, we could go home and sleep until whenever we wanted. Another very luxurious feature of that life. The freedom to eat and sleep, no matter how selfish and shallow, were part of the reason I was not in a hurry to start a family. As much as I didn't understand about motherhood, I did understand this: Once you have a kid, you *have* a kid, forever. All day.

I was very afraid to jump into the race of parenthood because of the knowns, the unknowns, and that for a long time I simply didn't see myself as the "type" to be a mother.

But now, with my two miracles, whose empty juice pouches litter the lawn, and their hardcore passion for all things cotton candy flavored, I get it. It's okay that most of my shirts have ketchup stains on them from where they held tight to give me a hug. And I am at peace with all of my washcloths being taken away, to then be used for stuffed animal blankets. The question of why on earth people put up with eating cold chicken nuggets has been answered for me in their sweet voices and abstract art. We're not crazy to live on fumes of sleep, resolve fights over who has more play-dough, read *Green Eggs and Ham* eight times in a row, or scrub the marker pictures off of a little brother. We are simply head over heels in love.

In the same way, non-runners simply don't understand our love of mileage—to them it looks as unpleasant as a mom sniffing her baby's diaper. Many times, in conversations with our non-running friends and family, they shake their heads and say, "I can't even *imagine* running thirteen miles, even if there was a cheeseburger being dangled in front of me." Knowing my audience, I love to instigate with a casual, "I only had a twelve-miler today."

They all become comedians, and one, without fail, will hold his beer, laugh heartily. "Heh – Heh! I don't even like to *drive* twenty-six miles, let alone run it!" Gee, we've never heard that one before. Even Chris Rock said it on Saturday Night Live before the 2014 New York City Marathon.

In 2009, we were having dinner with another couple, and David mentioned my upcoming second marathon, the one Ginny talked me into, and how proud he was. The other husband furrowed his eyebrows and asked why I was running another full, and he was a combination of confused and frustrated that my answer was a child-like, "It's fun!"

"Well, will you finish in the top ten?" he asked.

"Ummm, there will be about seventeen-thousand people in the race, so probably not..." I trailed off in a tone that indicated how much I thought it was a very dumb question.

"Well then, why bother if you aren't going to compete?" He really wanted to be right on this, but was certainly unclear on the meaning of the word "compete."

"Because it is a fun thing to run a marathon. It's a special day, and it's an accomplishment on its own. Do you win every golf match you play? Will you ever make it on the PGA tour? Probably not, but you still enjoy your sport," I challenged, with my second glass of courage.

"Well, golf is different. I'm always competing to win matches and get my score down."

"Same here. I like to do well for my age group and get my race times a bit faster."

"Oh, well then, I guess if you're trying to make a certain time, that's something."

That's something? He really didn't get it, and they *don't* get it if they've never done it, which is fine, because I'm not so sure I'd like to be packed in a corral with a guy like that.

We moved to Tampa, FL, from Buffalo, NY in 2001, and my longest race at that point was a 10-K, but since college, I had it in the back of my mind that someday I'd like to run a marathon. I remember our coaches talking about the Boston Marathon and its legendary runners. I could remember watching some of the New York City Marathon on television during high school and trying to imagine what on earth that would be like. It was a daunting idea, to say the least, but it was also thrilling to imagine being able to do it. Turning *imagining* into *believing* is of course, half the battle.

I set my sights on the 2003, Tenth Anniversary Walt Disney World Marathon. For one thing, we lived relatively close so travel would be easy and inexpensive. And, it was Disney—the ideal place to run a first marathon, with all of the passive entertainment and distraction from two-dozen plus miles of pain. I purchased Hal Higdon's *Marathon – The Ultimate Guide* (Rodale, 1999), read it over, and over, and over, and chose my plan. This training was a Big Deal. I purchased a cheerful new journal, colorful markers to write down my miles and workouts, and looked up pages of inspirational running quotes to write down with those colorful markers. I was following the plan with great ceremony and sacredness. It became a project of its own, a four-month hobby to liven up a predictable work-week.

Despite the excitement, I was scared. I read through the novice training plans, chose 'Novice 1,' and had my doubts about tackling such enormous amounts of miles. I kept looking for something more along the lines of a 'Novice Negative 5' plan. I needed to work up to a twenty-mile run? That was a lot. How long would that even take? But like having a baby, and having nine months to get used to that idea, I had a couple of months to let the excitement bubble up and smother the fear—fifteen weeks to work up to that first full twenty-miler. And as I patiently but steadily saw three miles turn into five, and then into eight, my courage grew with each week of training.

Even a tentative step forward in faith is rewarded with our capabilities sprinting forward.

I was working at a big university at the time and did much of my training on-campus right after work. Otherwise, by the time I sat through an hour of traffic and got home, it would be dark. And let's face it—walking into your house when it's dark and you're hungry after a long day of work can often bring on the temptation of run-skipping and cookie-scarfing. So, running with light and plenty of people around solved the issue of *when* I would do all of this running. Plus, by the time I finished, the traffic was cleared out and my commute home was smooth.

Some days, I would run during my lunch hour. Well, truth be told, "hour" is a bit of an understatement. Sometimes, I'd sneak in as much as ten miles, which took far longer than a flimsy hour. But no one seemed to notice, and if they did, they let it slide and gave me the very generous gift of looking the other way. I justified this extra time to my guilty conscience by the fact that a few of our staff members were outside smoking a lot, so once you added up the time for all of those smokes, I figured it was about the same, except that I smelled better and had more energy to get my work done. I cleaned myself up quite well in the women's restroom and kept a small hairdryer in my desk drawer. I was as fresh as a daisy the rest of the day.

Although I had been a runner since the spry age of eleven, I had no idea how tired I would be while grinding out miles in a marathon training program. Similar, I suppose, to those first few weeks and months of having a child. People constantly tell you how exhausted you'll be, but since you haven't hit the rock bottom of being among the walking-dead, you really don't understand. It's the kind of tired where you really have to stop and think, "Hmm, why do I have this cream cheese container in my hand, and how long has it been here?"

After my first twelve-mile run, I felt okay physically, but that afternoon I could barely keep my head up. I was at a birthday party for a one-year-old boy, the son of one of my friends. I sat quietly in a fluffy chair and people kept asking if I was all right. "Yes, fine, just a little tired is all. I'll get myself a glass of water and some cake." My eyes were the size of coin slots and I produced a steadily flowing river of yawns.

The exhaustion from the long runs did seem to get easier with each following marathon, which enabled me to do something other than lay on the couch barely coherent with my legs elevated.

These days, I can run fifteen miles like it's any other thing on my to-do list. "Ok, that three-hour run is done, time to get to the post office, pick up the dry cleaning, clean the house, and start dinner. Oh, gee, I hope I have time to shower before I pick up the kids."

Despite many following days of feeling worn out from work, travel, or landscaping, I stayed consistent with my training and missed only a handful of scheduled runs. Tired would have to wait until after the run was completed because it was a now-or-never kind of experience. If you didn't train now, you would hurt more later. Plus, as the idea of running a full marathon continued to court me, I fell more madly in love with it each day. "What's that Mr. Higdon, you think I should run seventeen miles today? Oh, okay..." Queue batting eyelashes. The rising excitement about my first marathon surprisingly gave a lot of needed motivation and energy, so *tired* would definitely lose.

We make many sacrifices for the things we really love.

Unfortunately, the one that kept winning was hunger. I really thought I'd shed a few pounds training for a marathon, but the amount of hunger made it almost impossible. I may have even put on a few pounds because the first time you tell your body to run that many miles, it's very confused, and it begs for more goodies. I also thought that the eight-miler made it legal, and possibly even necessary, to have a steak and cheese sub with onion rings. "I can eat whatever I want, I'm training for a marathon!" I danced around the house, using take-out menus for pom-poms. I later learned that I had that all wrong.

Needing plenty of hydration, I knew I would likely have to use a restroom during those long runs, so my routes always included a few strategically located gas stations. This regular use of gas station facilities was also great training for race day porta-potties, as well as for pregnancy. Your choices for restrooms are sometimes *very* traumatic. I tolerated the facilities as best as I could, and was able to pick up more water or Gatorade to finish up the last miles.

Race day finally came, and David drove me to the start line at 4:00 a.m., in what was essentially grid-lock. I couldn't help but wonder if I would make it to the start on time. REM's "Night Swimming" was on the radio, so whenever I hear that song now it brings back the memory of the butterflies in my stomach before my first marathon.

It was around forty degrees, quite cold by Florida standards, so I had gloves and throwaway layers to keep me warm. As I made the pilgrimage to the starting area under the towering streetlights, and through the maze of race tents and porta-potties, David made his way to the two-mile point. "Another One Bites the Dust" was blasting over the loudspeakers, a team favorite from high school cross-country, getting us pumped up for the firework start. When I saw Mickey Mouse at the top of a platform, felt the fireworks pound in my chest, and listened as everyone shouted, "Woooooooo!!!" I realized, "This is it. No time for fear, and no turning back. I have a job to do today, and it is to get across that finish line, even if I have to crawl."

Runners were packed in tightly on the narrow roads for the first few miles of that race, so it took me about five minutes to cross the start line and activate my chip timing. I saw David in the crowd of encouraging spectators at mile two, and pulled over to give him my extra layers. He cheered for me and off I went. I stopped for pictures with the characters, and a picture of the sunrise over Epcot. I also had two restroom stops, which were a time vacuum, but I was enjoying the race and wasn't worried about running a specific speed, other than hoping to finish it in under five hours.

The miles ticked by more quickly than I expected. Something that is also very hard to believe until you've done it. People look at you like there's something wrong with you when you tell them that a four-hour run really didn't seem like it was that long. I saw David again at about mile twenty-four, which was a great point to see a loved one, to help gather together what power you had left in the tank and see it through.

The people who love and support you are another kind of power gel more potent than the stuff in the package—they keep your heart in the race no matter what your calves are grumbling about.

The finish line of a first marathon is like no other. Neither one of us could believe what I had just done. We hugged, cheered, took some pictures, and knew it was a milestone. A life marker.

I proudly limped into the hotel, showered off a few layers of salt, and we went out for lunch, with me sporting my newly earned medal. After devouring a hefty cheeseburger, we began our drive home to Tampa, and *very* quickly, I fell asleep. Tired won this time. I was still rather sluggish the next few days, and since I felt as though my knees had been smashed with a sledgehammer, it was even difficult to sit down, so I just kind of had to land on couches and chairs. But I didn't mind, I had run a marathon.

Now that the marathon had been checked off my life list and we had been married a few years, settled in our jobs, we began to talk more realistically about starting a family. Approaching *this* start line was a huge unalterable decision, so I knew I had a lot to consider. It wasn't as simple as agreeing to show up for a fun-run. One of my first thoughts was that I lived twelve-hundred miles away from any of our family, and I had a husband that had a hefty collection of frequent flyer miles because of how often he traveled for his job. I was going to be on my own a lot. So just like a race, I was running with thousands of other people, but I was pretty much on my own two legs.

This was, *is*, our life though, and I rarely (generally only twice a year. You can ask David) complain, because I was and still am very grateful to be a stay-at-home mom. It's that same theme of racing for more time that seems to weave through running and every other area of our lives.

I realize it's not a dream job for some. Like the moms who wouldn't stay home even if they were paid twice what they were making, because not only do they love their career, but the thought of baby music classes instigates their gag reflex. The life of a stay-at-home mom sounds like a prison sentence of boredom and perpetually sticky floors. I can't exactly argue the point about the floors.

I know plenty of women who have intellectually fulfilling careers, great kids, and have been able to strike a healthy balance between their personal accomplishments and family life. For other moms, it's simply not financially possible to stay home for a few years, so they find ways to make everything work. The point is, we're all in the same race, just wearing different shoes.

I remind myself to have a lot of gratitude for my situation, despite the challenges and stickiness, and especially in the times when I question the choice to back away from a career path. I admire my friends with their positions of power and adventure, fancy suits and executive lunches, while I'm suited up in my uniform of khaki shorts and a frumpy T-shirt. Then I remember, some of us are good at the short races, and some of us are better at distance races. I take a look around my racecourse and again see that I registered for the right distance. I'll never be a

400-meter hurdler, so I better get a few minutes shaved off my half personal record (PR).

To help combat my lack of parenting knowledge, and prepare for this lifetime endurance event, I read a lot of the basic parenting books. Much in the same way I memorized Hal Higdon's *Marathon* book and waited anxiously for the new *Runner's World* issue each month. I hadn't been around babies in a very long time, so *What to Expect When You're Expecting* by Heidi Murkoff, Arlene Eisenberg, and Sandee Hathaway, B.S.N. (Workman Publishing, 2002) was the perfect type of book for me. I read a few similar titles that gave some accurate insight regarding what would happen to me, and what typical baby milestones would look like for the first few years.

One I continue to recommend is *Healthy Sleep Habits Healthy Child*, by Marc Weissbluth, (The Ballantine Publishing Group, 1999). I loved, and still love, routine. And I became a huge fan of being on a nap schedule. The naps were the mile markers for our day and benefitted both of us. I not only had a happy child as the book promised, but I had regular time during the day to catch up on my calls, cleaning, e-mails, a workout, or reading, knowing she'd be sleeping for a bit—I knew my break was coming. Plus, I loved that illusion of control, it was very calming for me, but often absent in parenting, and I grasped at whatever I could to get my fix.

Having a predictable schedule also gave me a sense of purpose in filling our days. For special events and travel, we'd mess with the naps a bit, but most of our daily activities fit with the schedule. Things like story time at the library, playgroups at the park, and music classes all fit in with the naps. If this sounds a lot like training for a race, it sure was. The baby was happier when she napped, the mommy was happier when she ran.

It's very simple really—once you know when you're getting that run in, when you know your time is coming, everything else just falls into place. Having a training plan, both at home and on the road, has helped me get through thousands of long miles.

I didn't know as a twelve-year-old that I would *love* running, just as we really don't realize how much we are going to *love* our child. It is completely new territory, and all of those people, men included, that tell a woman that she won't believe how much she will love her child—they are all correct, every single one of them. What we learn from babies, *and* a good run, is that love is far more powerful than being tired.

Even though the night feedings have a terrible reputation, I realized what a sweet and fleeting time it really was, so love won and tired had to wait. Holding her tiny, warm back wrapped in soft cotton jammies, looking into her dark, concentrating eyes with only a night-light casting a golden glow, and hearing her deep breathing was very calming. But I knew these moments wouldn't last forever. Morning always came, and even though it might have been Saturday, formerly known as *the weekend*, and I'd rather sleep a while longer, I got up and didn't mind. I had a baby.

Chapter 3
Marathon Training? Pregnancy? Feels About the Same

If you were a runner before being pregnant, you probably know what I mean. Although running usually feels great, and helps us feel great on a daily basis, there are times when it is uncomfortable or causes some aches and pains. Sometimes, you're too tired, it's too hot, too cold, too rainy, your nagging injury is having a temper tantrum, or you have a full- blown injury keeping you off the roads. But even though it hurts sometimes, we keep plugging away, and we always end up happy that we got our miles in for the day.

Upon comparing the running books and the pregnancy books, there is one major difference: You have *far* more control over your running. The race training books tell you how much to run on any given day, ideas about what to eat and how to safely stretch your aching parts. But the pregnancy books tell you what's going to happen to you, no matter what you have to say about it, and how much you are going to stretch without your consent. No control here ladies. You can't run your five-miler on Tuesday instead of Thursday. Life just keeps going, and growing, without your meddling. "This week, your baby is the size of a walnut, and expect to see your belly button pop out like the Thanksgiving turkey is done." *Eww.* "This week, your precious baby is the size of a grapefruit and you have constant flatulence." *Uggh.*

Runners are encouraged to take a day or two off of running per week during periods of intense training, while pregnant women still have to go to work and take care of other small children, and they can't take a day or two off of being pregnant. "Ahhh, that's better. I can wear that cute skirt today, and paint my own toenails. I'll be pregnant again tomorrow once I'm caught up with the weeding and get the garage cleaned out."

Like training, pregnancy is similar in that there is a start and a finish in a set period of weeks. There is plenty of discomfort, a lot of really bad smells, endless eating, and piles of laundry. You plug away, knowing it won't last forever, and at the end of the training there is a fun race, a shiny medal, and a banana, maybe a slice of pizza, the perfect reward for all your hard efforts. The preggos get a cute baby to cuddle after their training is complete.

As a mom *and* a runner, I found myself eating things I never would have thought possible. While pregnant, I had Happy Meals as a "snack" to soothe my queasy stomach, but when running, I became queasy after squirting sticky slime from energy gel packets into my mouth. The mom has low-back pain, the runner has black toenails, six of one, half-dozen of the other.

Being able to recognize the joys in the training, and in the pregnancy, despite the aches and pains, adds to the appreciation of both the medal, and the baby. Sure, finishing a marathon isn't quite the same miracle as producing a small human, but both are big celebrations of our strength, and the start of the post-race party.

My pregnancies overall were very easy, but I had a lot of nausea in the first trimesters for both kids—worse with the second. It was so awful that I couldn't eat or drink anything and keep it down. With my face in various shades of green, I dragged myself through the beverage aisles of grocery stores and tried every liquid out there, but they always came back up. I was losing weight, which of course is not the goal when you're pregnant. My doctor gave me an anti-nausea medication, and that took the edge off. Fortunately, by week fourteen, just as quickly as it started, the nausea disappeared. Then all I wanted was chicken wings, onion rings, and steaks. I kept saying, "I think it's a girl, but it seems to eat like a man!" As it turned out, he was in fact a boy.

As you try to get through your day carrying around empty plastic bags "just in case," having tiny feet jammed up in your rib cage, and needing to stop at every restroom you pass, you still know that you have another mile in you. You get in your mental zone, tap into your super-power to push beyond the discomfort, and you can get through another day.

To this day I don't know if it is true or a myth, but I remember hearing talk about a woman's feet stretching and growing up to a *full* size bigger after being pregnant. As if all the other parts stretching like silly putty wasn't enough. This possibility scared me more than all the other unpleasant side effects. While I'll admit that during a training period my feet can look a little frightening, I was happy with my feet the way they were, and in no hurry to have to move up a size. It didn't matter that my butt grew because I knew it would eventually go back to normal, but once feet are stretched out, there's no going back. To be on the safe side of the myth, I kept my legs elevated whenever I possibly could. When I was still working, I slanted my body at my desk and set up a little homemade ottoman in hopes of keeping my feet the same size. Whether that was the trick, or I was just plain lucky I don't know, but my feet did not get bigger.

For runners, feet pose all sorts of discussions about blisters, great socks, tendon injuries, and lost toenails. At least when we go running-shoe shopping, those people know what they are in for, and know exactly what we're hiding in our arch support socks. We don't have to explain or apologize. But shopping for pretty shoes, some special occasion dainty pair, we know that those sales people aren't always so accustomed to the visual reality that awaits them.

I passed through a department store and saw the perfect pair of sparkly high-heeled sandals to go with a dress that I already owned for an upcoming event. *I am powerless against just the right amount of sparkle.* I was hesitant to try them on because I knew I didn't even have polish on my toes, so this could be a bit embarrassing. But the nice salesman brought them out and I carefully unwrapped the crisp white tissue from the box, then I began slipping them on while he went to help another customer. I stood up to take a look in the mirror at the artwork on my feet when he came back to ask, "How do you like the shoes?"

"Oh, they are so pretty," I replied. "I think they're perfect, but please don't look too closely. I run a lot and you may not want to see what that can do to a foot."

"Oh, don't be silly." He glanced down. "Oh. I see. Will you be taking these home today?" he asked, hoping I would, and not just to pad his commission.

"Yes, please." I knew that when the time came, and with a bit of polish, my feet would look just fine for those lovely shoes.

The worst thing I ever faced during a pregnancy didn't have anything to do with my feet. I was pregnant with my first child and had some issues, but I rarely complained because even though my head was regularly in the toilet, I thought it was cute that I was living the whole cliché. So, I tried to find the humor in it and enjoy each chapter, knowing the finish line was just up ahead...past the saltines. Plus, I enjoyed my daily visits with fun-sized chocolate bars, and people *typically* let pregnant women cut in line for pretty much everything.

It was around week thirty-eight that I noticed itchy red

patches developing around the elevation maps of stretch marks on my tummy. They spread to my arms and legs too. I was covered, and I mean *covered*. Constant. Itching. Living in Florida, I could spend a lot of time in the pool, and that kept me fairly comfortable. I tried all sorts of things—calamine, witch hazel, you name it, but nothing ever made the itching completely stop.

It's called PUPPP, which stands for Pruritic Urticarial Papules and Plaques for Pregnancy. The more informal term is, "Oh My Goodness Gracious I'm Going to Go Insane from This Itching!" It is surprisingly common in first pregnancies, but rarely reoccurs in later ones. That was a piece of good news.

The *bad* thing about living in Florida is that this took place in 2004, the year we had a parade of hurricanes passing through, so for about a week it wasn't safe to be in the pool. I filled the tub with oatmeal baths and basically lived there. I had books, snacks, and music next to me to keep busy. At a checkup close to the due date, the doctor saw my agony, and with no sign of the baby vacating the premises, we decided to pick a day for eviction—a week after the official due date. I hoped my super-power of mental endurance would come in handy, and that I could handle a couple more itchy miles.

The last leg of the ultra-marathon known as pregnancy is of course delivery. You know the finish line is ahead, but you're also unsure of the route, or how much more this might hurt. Doubt begins to creep in. "I'm not so sure I'll be able to do this. I can see more crowds of people, so I must be getting close, but it sure feels like my legs are going to slip like wet noodles into the road cracks." Even the most brave of us can feel our legs fall apart, bolt by bolt at this point.

Audrey was being induced, which I was a little uncomfortable with because after eating bags and bags of fun-sized Snickers and watching TLC's *A Baby Story*, there seemed to be a strong correlation between induction and C-section. Surprise,

surprise, Audrey's heart rate was diving. They stopped the Pitocin, and it leveled out for a few hours, but eventually the doctors said, "We can't wait any longer. We're moving you into a room for an emergency C-section." All I could think was, "Uh-oh, I am going to be sliced open with a knife. I have to get in my zone. Are there any running shoes around here?"

Thanks to the epidural and possibly some calming potion in my IV, much of that afternoon was a blur, as well as the ride to the delivery room. David has said that I was hilarious and was convinced I was on an NFL team, heading out to the field, but I have no recollection of any of this.

One night during this first pregnancy, we were having dinner at our coffee table in the family room. While watching Seinfeld reruns, David turned to me and said, "What do you think about *not* finding out if the baby is a boy or girl?"

I looked at him like he was from another century and said, "No way! I'm dying to know. So we'll know how to decorate, and what to register for." We talked about it for a while, and even though it was certainly not what I planned, I saw how it would be like a little game and add to the fanfare of breaking the tape. Of course, it drove everyone around us crazy because it simply wasn't common to wait until the big day anymore, again because of the decorating and baby shower registries. That was easy though. I found bedding of animals, with fuzzy giraffes and monkeys in perfect soothing colors. I was content with lots of yellow and green outfits. *I'm not really a saver of things, but I still have all this.* The great thing about the neutral colors, we were able to use all the bedding and newborn clothes again with our second child, Ethan, who we also waited until the big day to find out the gender of. It was such a sweet thing, and I wouldn't have had it any other way.

But back to this trip down the hospital corridor. I knew my super-power would help me refrain from freaking out, despite the fact that I was going to be gutted like a fish. I focused on this family milestone of having our first child, and I got into my zone. And all I remember next is hearing them say, "It's a girl!"

Through joyful tears, we were laughing and celebrating the birth of our first child. I was humiliatingly strapped to a table with my arms tied down and out to my sides, as if they suspected I was going to grab the kid and run out of there. So, David got to see her first, and he made the final call on the name. We were torn between Audrey and Hannah, but he just knew. Then he held her near me so I could see her little face for the very first time. The joy, the pounding heart, the cheering, the feeling of your chest bursting open as you crossed the finish line—it was magic.

So, when's the next race? I'm in.

Chapter 4
Runners Don't Need Much Gear, But Kids Sure Do!

Moms have seemingly bottomless bags. Ask a mom for an umbrella, a change of clothes, superglue or fresh batteries and she probably has it in her bag. Always armed with drinks, snacks, first-aid kit and even an extra set of flip flops because Ethan often left home without shoes, I was prepared for anything

Sometimes the technology and new-fangled products that are intended to make our lives easier, only add to the to-do list. I can just as easily look at a map for three minutes instead of fiddling with the car navigation system for twenty minutes. The dishwasher is my pal, my teammate when I load it up, but then it just sits there when I have to empty it. When they make a dishwasher that can empty itself, then maybe I'll be *really* impressed. I'll admit that the one household gadget that I may have an inappropriate relationship with is my steam cleaner. This thing is awesome. Go ahead, spill a coffee, or run through with muddy shoes. I can make it disappear in a jiffy!

A lot of baby gear is more work than it is helpful. For example, the one thing I wish I had skipped is the fancy diaper pail. The bags were expensive, they never tore off correctly, and the only similarity that it had to being "Outdoor Fresh Scented" was that it often smelled like the elephant habitat at the zoo when it was time to empty it. It was a nuisance, and I remember when we chose to stop using it all together, but forgot to tell our babysitter. For days I kept thinking, "What is that awful smell and where is it coming from?!" It's amazing what one wet diaper can do after a few days. I bravely removed the bag with the one offensive diaper, and sprayed the entire unit with a powerful bleach cleaning spray. The smell was still there. I submerged the entire pail into the pool for a few days thinking the chlorine would kill it. After all, kids occasionally peed in the pool, and chlorine killed the pee, so that sounded like good math. But the smell remained. The fancy diaper pail's next move was to the curb. It was not a helpful gadget.

Like it or not, you really do need a lot of stuff to care for this tiny person. The bouncy seat, the highchair, the pack-n-play, the car seat, the stroller, the saucer, the diaper bag, the mat where they lay on their back and swat at the hanging toys, etc., etc. The relief came when they got bigger and we had less gear to lug around. After all, what's more fun than packing all this stuff and adding to the already exciting game of Airline Travel? "Congratulations, Scott family! You are the lucky winners of a two-hour delay and one-hour luxury stay on the tarmac. You will be the envy of all your friends as you report your destroyed luggage and lost phone. Better have plenty of diapers and formula in that already stuffed bag! Have a great trip!"

Ignorance really did give us a false sense of courage when we went to New York City one fall with a doublewide stroller. Yes, the locals just adored us as we awkwardly crossed streets and ordered lunches at restaurants with that stroller we lovingly called "the tank." The really surprising thing was that a few drugstores and a fast-food restaurant were two stories high and didn't have elevators. On Monday, David had a meeting, so there I was finding a parking space for the stroller, strapping on the big bag, carrying the small child while holding the hand of the big child, climbing the stairs to order breakfast, and carrying it all back to a table. I felt so glamorous hanging out in the Big Apple.

What made this trip all worthwhile was, after the kids and I survived breakfast, we walked over to where the *Today Show* was aired. The show that had been my morning company after Audrey was born—my life-line to the rest of the world. It was a Monday and not very crowded, so I parked the double-wide, circled the fences like a puma, and finally found a spot up close. I held Ethan in my arms, and Audrey was standing next to me as I excitedly pointed out the people from the show. A sweet woman next to me asked where we were from, how old the kids were, and was very friendly. She then said the best thing, "Stay here, they know me, Al Roker will come and say hello to you." I thought, "They *know* you?" So, of course I stayed firmly planted. Sure enough, Al Roker asked Audrey her name, and I told him Ethan's, and we were on the Today Show for a few seconds. Ginny happened to be watching it that morning and went bananas when she saw us on live TV! She recorded it, as she had the same morning friendship with that show at her house. I thanked that kind woman like crazy.

Right after our brief moment of stardom, we went into the NBC shop and I picked up a few small souvenirs to commemorate the occasion, particularly this cool pair of *Today Show* pajama shorts that I still wear. They make me think of that surprising little moment every time. What are the odds? I love that Audrey still remembers it too.

The mothers who are raising children in big cities get extra respect. You win. I think I'm tough, independent and capable, and then there's *you*. The manual labor of getting from point A to point B is so exhausting. I suppose they modeled the Tough Mudder races after your experiences. "Okay Ladies, after you run through the flames, you have to carry two twenty-pound children through randomly slamming subway doors, dodge speeding bicycles while retrieving dropped binkies, and carry a week's worth of groceries up five flights of stairs. Here's your medal!"

It was a relief to start shedding the gear and be able to travel light, both daily, and for longer trips. One summer, we were on a beach vacation. The kids were five and three, walking on a wooden path to the sand. David and I were holding each other's hand like in the olden days. As we watched the kids walk ahead of us, it occurred to us that it was the first summer without begging a stroller to move through deep, powdery sand, and we got to hold hands with each other! Ahh, the load was getting lighter.

The toys are overpowering our home, though. I try to clean them out every so often, but it's still rather ridiculous. Between the relatives, the birthday parties, and Santa, there is just so much stuff in the house. Oftentimes, as the kids are opening gifts, I quickly move things out of sight, knowing that although it looks very exciting right now, these things will never see a minute of play. This pile then gets split between the consignment shop and the re-gift pile. The owner of the consignment shop once asked me, "Don't you let your kids open *any* gifts?!" Between the school day, playing outside all winter, and swimming all summer, there isn't much time left for playing indoors. Plus, there's the iPads. I have a mixed relationship with them. Yes, I can make dinner in peace, but I think *actual* pudding is leaking out of their heads where their brains used to be. Everything in moderation. Right?

The sports equipment is just as bad. They outgrow bikes and roller blades, and even golf clubs become too short as their bodies grow taller. And for some reason, we can't resist buying yet *another* bouncy ball. "Mommy, pleeease! Can I get this bouncy ball? I *always* wanted the blue/striped/bumpy/Pooh Bear one!" Ethan will ask every time we are in Target.

"Okaaay," I resign again because it's an outdoor toy, knowing they'll be outside getting plenty of exercise. I bet if I collected them from all corners of the house and garage, I could set up our very own ball pit and charge admission, which would help pay for the next size of bikes.

Even though I clean out and get rid of things, there are some things I save. The physical items that I hold, sniff, and see memories in. A few baby toys in particular that Audrey, and later Ethan, and I played with over and over, sitting on the carpet together. The Elmo shape sorter for one, with Elmo squeakily rewarding each correct shape match with a big "Hooraaay!" And these stacking musical pots that, for some reason, the kids just loved as babies. I'm so glad I was able to sit with them and play, which is what makes these toys more than garage sale stock. They show me the pictures in my head of what they looked like at eight months, or sixteen months, and what it felt like to hold them and smell their hair. There we are, simply playing, smiling, with nothing else to worry about, or nothing more important to do in those swiftly striding moments.

Some more childhood gear is their *security* gear. We received a yellow stuffed duck at one of the baby showers. We had a few stuffed animals placed in the crib, and Audrey chose Ducky as her pal early on. She used him as a pillow, and he went everywhere with us. I was able to order a few more online to rotate them out for washing and equal wear, and to have as back-ups in case of an emergency. So, we had four identical ducks.

Ducky even receives clothes from Santa for Christmas. Whatever outfit or costume she thinks up, Santa miraculously delivers. It started with a spacesuit, then a scuba suit, Santa suit, and character costumes from *Toy Story,* and even *Peter Pan's* leafy green getup.

David, Audrey, and Ethan were out one day when I received

the call that every mother dreads. I picked up the ringing phone. "Hello!"

"Hi Honey, it's me. We're at Lowe's and we lost Ducky," David told me nervously.

"Well, you have to find him. Do not leave that store without Ducky. Where were you? Go to every single place you were in the store and look under every shelf. Did you take her to the restroom?"

"Yes, and I've checked there already. I've checked everywhere very carefully. I can't find him," said the man who can rarely locate the butter in the fridge.

"You said you were looking at garden hoses, so go check all through there. Anywhere she may have climbed."

"I did that already, no luck," he said.

"How is Audrey?? Will she even leave there without him? Is she upset?"

"Yes, but I told her the people who work here will find him and we'll come back for him later," he answered.

I was not on board with this plan. I wanted them to find Ducky, but I said, "Okay, I'll get a spare Ducky out and tell her that they were delivering plants in the neighborhood and dropped him off while they were near our house."

"Got it, thanks."

I called that store every day for a week, and the woman who kept taking my call did not appreciate my tenacity. *I realize now that I should have called at different times during the day to get a different person.* She finally made it clear that they had looked everywhere, and if they found the duck they would call us. Obviously, she had no idea that Ducky was a man of great importance and respect in his community. I continued to sneak in, searching, hoping, but I finally had to accept the fact that he was gone. We had only three Duckys left.

The good news is, no more have been lost, and we still have the original Ducky. Ducky has had stuffing added and removed, as well as a prosthetic ankle attached. Most recently, he has had both feet replaced. Audrey picked out the fabric and we prepped him for surgery. He was a great patient. Ducky has been growing up right along with Audrey, and like the way we mark the kids' heights on the wall of the pantry every six months, Audrey has measured Ducky on the wall of her closet. He has outgrown his toy car seat and now uses only a seatbelt, like a big kid. Ducky has also expanded his musical tastes, from Laurie Berkner, to Austin & Ally, and to One Direction—a change I am not sure I am ready for. Ducky lives a very full life, and I'm sure he will bring us a lot more excitement in the coming years.

We made a discovery about Ethan on that memorable trip to New York City. He was just under a year old at the time, and we packed a few of his small stuffed toys for him to hold. This one little Pooh Bear beanie was like a relaxation spell. Anytime he cried or fussed, we handed him the Pooh Bear and he immediately took it and put his thumb in his mouth. We had so much fun with this at first because it really was like a little magic trick.

He also has a small stuffed ladybug, so together they are known as Pooh and Lip. *Lip was short for ladybug long before a little kid could say the word ladybug.* They have also traveled everywhere with us, and babysitters are told that, aside from the kids themselves, Ducky, Pooh, and Lip are the three most important things to keep an eye on.

Ethan was struggling to quit his thumb-sucking habit after he turned seven, and he was wise enough to know that if Pooh and Lip were removed, so was his thumb. He was right. He let Pooh and Lip stay in the family room when he went to bed, and that was it. He quit cold turkey. *Brave boy, you did it. It's all mental.*

Photographs and scrapbooks are the gear we can use to get a little time-travel in. Since everyone tells you how tired you'll be, how much you'll love your child, and how fast the time flies, you have to take a lot of pictures. That being said, I am not a scrap booker. I'm *really* not. My brother's wife is extremely talented with this art form, but this genetic trait didn't even look my way. I actually complain out loud each time I sit down to update these things because it is a lot of work, but I have made a scrapbook for each of the kids for each year since their birth until about age ten. They are not fancy—the kids could probably have done better themselves—but they are a visual record of their growth, their activities, and exciting adventures through each year. Audrey will occasionally get in a phase of wanting to read through only scrapbooks at bedtime, instead of storybooks.

Photographs are the trails to revisit our mile markers. How in the world was this flag-football-playing, backpack-carrying little man ever seven pounds seven ounces?? What happened?? That, of course, is why people keep having babies, so they can experience that wonderful smallness again and pour all of their love into that softly breathing little butterball. Just like when you see your race pictures, you get the uncontrollable urge to find another race to sign up for so you can once again hold that magic.

The pictures of our kids reveal all the progress they made in such a short period of time, and all the progress *we* made right along with them. After all, I don't know about you, but I was not, and am still not, a perfect mom. Some days I look more like a mother vulture than Mother Goose. The pictures, however, remind us of some of the happiest moments we had. One of my favorites is a picture of Audrey at about ten months old, sitting on the grass laughing so hysterically that you can almost hear it. All I was doing was saying "ick" and "guk," and strange made-up words. And that was all it took for the fits of uncontrollable laughter. It seems the pictures of the unexpected moments end up being the ones we cherish over the posed pre-k graduation ones. Those are cute, but they don't tell the stories of our special bonds like the unplanned photos.

Audrey had one other piece of security gear, and that was: notes. Into fourth grade, she wanted a note in her lunchbox every single day. If we had a babysitter at night, she expected a bedtime note. During summer vacation, if I got up to run before David and the kids were up, I often left her a note on the couch, where she would slowly wake up with a cup of juice and her favorite shows.

The written word of affection and simple humor is so important to her. I have a large collection of these tiny notes written on scraps of construction paper, or leftover notebook paper that represent what movies we were into, games we played, trips we took, jokes we made, and even apologies for arguments we had. Like a training journal recording our miles, weather, speed and injuries, the evidence of our love is all in the notes.

After a few days away from home, visiting family in our hometowns, I followed David and the kids into the house and asked, "Why does it smell like very old cat litter in here? Did someone get a cat and not tell me?"

"I know, right?" David looked at me like he was thinking the exact same thing.

"Eww, what is it? Can you tell where it's coming from?" I asked from the kitchen as I set down the backpacks from the plane ride.

"Not really, but it's going away a little bit," he replied as he went back out to the car for more luggage.

I went through the entryway from the garage a few times and realized that was the location of the offensive smell. Our washer and dryer were along this route, as well as the utility sink. I checked in the sink and saw a lot of gravel from the fish tank, so I figured that's what it was. I turned on the water to rinse out the sink and continued unpacking. The car now unpacked and the door to the garage closed, I brought the clothes to the washing machine and smelled it again. I looked in the garbage can, thinking it would be more gravel from cleaning out the fish tanks, but no gravel. In fact, nothing was in the garbage. Out of the corner of my eye, I turned to look at the small, three-shelf wire unit and saw five pairs of my running shoes trying to look innocent, just casually chatting with the flip-flops, and I just knew. "Who? Us?" they seemed to ask me.

"Sorry honey, it was me," I fessed up. "It's my running shoes. They smell like a litter box. I'll bring them outside and air them out."

Always a comedian, he made a comment about my sport of choice and the silly number of shoes it required. His favorite movie is *Forrest Gump*, so he thinks all we need is that one pair of Nike's from the 1980's and we're good to go. I had to rise to the defense of us all and explain why we have so many pairs of running shoes, knowing he wouldn't quite buy it. He also doesn't buy the advice that they need to be replaced after approximately three to five hundred miles, more or less, because it's just a "scam" to sell more shoes. Let's go count his golf clubs. *Tee-hee.*

But you know that we have our basic trainers, maybe two pairs that we alternate between. It's nice to have a lighter model, or even a racing model. If you are lucky enough to live near cool trails, then you have at least one pair of trail-running shoes. All the retired ones have new jobs now, like the yardwork pair and the grocery shopping pair. I even have an old black pair of Brooks that work well as boots if we have to go up north in the winter months. I look at it this way—I am recycling my running shoes for new uses, and thus saving him bundles of money by not purchasing "grocery shopping shoes." It's so clear to me.

During my teen years, we didn't have a lot of disposable income. My parents were divorced, and I lived with my mom who often worked two jobs to keep us afloat. So, the idea of spending ninety dollars on a pair of running shoes was close to the equivalent of a month or more of groceries at the time. This being the reason why I lost my size-and-a-half-too-big shoes in the mud. My fifteen-year-old brain came up with this: I'll get the best I can for the least amount of money. *Oh, wait. I still do that.* But that day, the best for the least were too big, so I figured I'd wear extra socks, tie them up well, and no one would know the difference. We all know how that turned out.

I saved whatever money came my way from birthdays, good report cards, babysitting, delivering newspapers, anything. Once I had saved enough, my mom drove me to a running store so I could purchase my first pair of Nike Air shoes. Remember when the little window through the sides of the sole just came out? That was an exciting time for running shoes, and we all wanted them, not caring for a second that it may have been a very cool marketing ploy. I was on top of the world, like reaching for the hope diamond itself, the running shoe carefully placed on the golden pedestal and the light sparkling on it just so. I clutched that shoebox containing the white shoes with light green trim very tightly, and all was right with the world. I continued to work whatever jobs I could find within walking distance because when you love something so much, all the sacrifice is worth it.

I still love going to buy new running shoes. They all look so clean and fast. So perfectly lined up on the display walls with the lights shining on them to bring out their natural sparkle. I am intoxicated by the "new running shoe smell." I get giddy with excitement when trying on some new models of old favorites that were just born. They are still so pure, without rips from trails, or pebbles lodged in the tread, or the smell of ammonia. I love going to my locally owned running store and being around other runners. It's part of the shopping experience. Toss in some new socks, complete with functioning elastic, and my day is made. Although, they might cringe when they see my car pull up. "Here comes that mom who's always in the khaki shorts and way too excited about new shoes. You take her, Mike." The only thing that can make that shopping trip better is if I have a coupon.

To help speed up your new running shoes, many of you run with music. I haven't done that since Marky Mark and the Funky Bunch were belting out "Good Vibrations" back in college. In the early 1990's, we had gigantic Walk-mans that held cassette tapes and came with floppy, foam-covered earphones that constantly fell off. The wires randomly disconnected, and you had to swat them back into functioning. Since the fitness magazines were starting to advise women to run without headphones so they could hear potential muggers, it was an easy choice to leave that irritant at home. I was attending college in an urban environment, and I didn't have cider mills or duck-crossing signs on my routes anymore. Instead, there were convenience stores with bars over the windows, expressway entrances, and bus stops. It was smart to be aware of my surroundings in order to hear traffic, dogs, cyclists, and other people. Without music, I learned to love and rely on the sounds of nature, the neighborhood, and the rhythm of my own breathing and cadence.

Most of my friends rely on their music to pump them up, and I get that. I love hearing some good tunes blaring out at a race, and I can get some good songs in my head if I need to, but I never missed having it for every run, and to this day I run without it. And since I'm a little slow when it comes to obtaining new technology products, I certainly don't miss lugging around that brick of a Walk-man.

My running gear remains very simple. I spend my big running dollars on good shoes and good sports bras. I do like a nice cushy sock too. Otherwise, most of my running clothes are inexpensive and utilitarian, most of my shirts are the ones given out at races. But when it comes to sports bras, women have so many better options than thirty years ago for maximum support. Yes, good bras cost a lot, but are absolutely worth every penny. You'll be much more comfortable when *they* are strapped in, unable to speak freely. It's like a time-out of sorts. Look at it like the pack-n-play—when Audrey and Ethan were very little, we kept them in it outside by the pool. They can play, but they need to be packed so everyone can have fun and be safe.

My gear also includes a GPS watch. Knowing my distance and pace is really cool. Before this little gadget, I was wearing a ten-dollar drugstore watch, and measuring miles with the car. This watch was ten minutes slow, and the buttons were so messed up that I couldn't even fix the time. But let's face it, after all those years of running, you can take a pretty good guess at how far you've run, just by how long you've been out there.

I always wear a running cap to keep my hair and the sun out of my eyes. Plus, I like the feeling of privacy it gives me. I have a Road ID on my shoe or watch band on the off chance I take a mid-run nap in someone's yard. During the school year, I run after morning drop-off. So, in order to keep my phone with me in case there is a monkey bar incident at school, I pack it in my running belt, with a couple of dollars and the car key.

Before the 2013 Chicago Marathon, David presented me with a very thoughtful gift to celebrate the occasion. He got a new, more modern running belt to carry my things in because, on the long runs with extra weight in the belt from GU Chomps and raisins, the old one often chafed so badly that I'd have scrapes and scabs, and feel stinging pain in the shower. But, since I am a bit frugal, I just lived with it and didn't want to spend the money on a new one. I opened this wonderful new belt, thanked him profusely, and told him not to be offended but I couldn't use it for the race. I felt terrible seeing the disappointed look in his eyes, and I reassured him that I loved his gift. It was so thoughtful and generous, and it truly touched my heart.

But the fact is this: *Nothing New On Race Day.* This rule can never be vetoed, no matter whose feelings are at stake. I didn't plan to wear my old belt either. I carry nothing that won't fit in my bra, other than a water bottle in my hand, but I'm used to that. I told him that if I had to fidget with that thing mid-race, or started to feel chafing from it, I'd have to leave it on the side of the road. He had a look of horror on his face at that comment, like he and his gift were personally attacked. But sure enough, there were plenty of discarded running items along the course, and I was glad none of them were my new belt. As soon as I started back to running after Chicago, I've been using it ever since, and it doesn't chafe!

We do get torn up a bit on these long runs, so I also like a stick of Body Glide to use in spots that I expect will get some friction for runs ten miles or more. I can't help but giggle at the name though, and my non-running friends love it when I talk about Body Glide at parties. It provides the opening for a multitude of jokes. Tubes of Icy Hot or Bio Freeze are always in my supplies, too. The smell of menthol and wet leaves automatically brings me to the start line of a race. Aromatherapy for runners.

I really need to use sunblock each and every time I head out. The Florida sun is not something to be underestimated, and us locals can always spot the out-of-towners in December—they are the only ones burnt to a crisp. They warned us when we were teenagers, slippery with baby oil on silver mats, but we just didn't believe them. I am starting to see evidence of years of sun damage speckling my arms, hands, and of course, face. So now, in my car I keep a stick for my face, and a spray for anything else that the sun can touch.

We actually do require some cold weather gear in Florida. Can anyone give a shout-out for the 2010 Walt Disney World Marathon? This was the one that I let Ginny talk me into. The half on Saturday provided sleet for the runners, and the marathon on Sunday was not much better—twenty-nine degrees, never exceeding thirty-five. I felt bad for those who travelled from cold climates to enjoy some warmer weather. It certainly wasn't warm that particular weekend.

For that race, buses leave the hotels starting at 3:00 a.m. and it takes a while to get through the traffic, so you're outside for close to two hours before the first wave of runners get going. As we clean out our closets during the year, I keep a stash of throw-away clothes in a separate pile, and I encouraged Ginny well in advance to look around her and her husband's closet for things she might be willing to wear to the start line but then leave on the side of the road as she warmed up. She and I had plenty of layers that day, and even two old fleece blankets that I brought. But since it was so bitterly cold, we threw away very little.

When the first waves finally started moving forward, we followed along to the start line and leaped over clumps of blankets and sweatshirts. Water cups dropping to the ground created patches of ice around the water stations. I really don't think I could feel my feet until about mile three. It was like slamming wooden planks against the ground. In my finish line picture, there is a guy wearing shorts, and I can feel the cold just looking at him.

Good tights, good gloves, and a nice windbreaker are a must around here for the cold days. I'll wear a warm hat that covers my ears, and I love to put pieces of cotton balls in my ears to keep the wind out.

Training for that particular race, I had enough time in the morning to run before David left for work, and I had to get the kids off to pre-school. I got up a little after 6:00 a.m. and was able to get up to ten miles in on some days, but usually no more than six. It was dark for most of those runs, but as the Florida sun came up, it did start to warm a bit, so I tossed layers at the end of my driveway during loops around the neighborhood. I could shed layers, and even got to keep them at the end.

Cold weather gear is also essential for trips to the northern part of the country, where we visit family who still live up there. Prior to visiting my family in Virginia in early February, I asked my sister-in-law about the weather conditions, and packed what I thought was appropriate. She mentioned that it would be in the high fifties, but I forgot to ask what the lows would be. After dinner the first night of my stay, we drove to my mom's house, and I realized it was just below thirty degrees. That meant that when I got up to get a few miles in, it would be absolutely freezing! Panic set in when I realized that, although I packed great gear, including gloves, a windbreaker, scarf, and a few long sleeve shirts, I did not pack my running tights or the dark blue winter running hat that makes me look like a bank-robber, but does a great job covering my ears. The lack of one simple pair of tights could never stop me from enjoying a run in different surroundings than my usual routes at home, so I put on all my gear and wore my khaki pants from the day before, which became my temporary running pants for the trip. I had my running cap, and stuffed cotton in my ears, but the cold was so biting that five minutes into the run I wrapped my scarf around my head and tied it under my chin to cover any exposed skin. Looking a lot like one of my Polish relatives wearing her kerchief, I happily ran my five-milers. *We will always find a way to get our fix.*

Having such small gear is a great feature for a runner. Wherever you go, you can always take your sport with you and fit your gear in a suitcase, or small bag. Like a baby in an infant car seat carrier, it's so completely portable. My daughter is into hockey, which requires her to have so much equipment attached to her tiny body. Plus, you need a specific place for her sport, but she doesn't mind. I always tell her she should be a runner - all you really need to get a run in is a good pair of shoes and a good bra.

We multiply our gear with the trinkets we pick up at a race, or a race expo. It's not just a coffee mug. It's a time machine back to the race. The shirts, the reusable grocery bags, and the water bottles are parts of our story, the proof of what we accomplished. And like the tiny footprints from the hospital, the attempt to hold on to that fleeting magical day.

On my way to run the Chicago Marathon in 2013, I planned it more like a hunting expedition than anything else. I wanted to come back with as much as possible with the race logo. If they made oven mitts with the logo, I'd get them. That expo was enormous, and we did a lot of shopping. I came back with a few shirts, a jacket, a hat, and a *jillion* of the square Bank of America Magnets, but I never could locate the oven mitts.

Photographs at races are big business, and like our family pictures that show us where we've been, how far we've come, and how ridiculous we have looked. I'll do the posed one at the finish line, holding up my medal, but it's not going to be the one I order in the end. I love the gritty, sweaty, focused ones, where I'm clearly just running and not trying to look any certain way. The pictures that show the salty sweat lines on your face, and your slightly crooked gait, exposing fatigue setting in, are the real storytellers, and they don't sugarcoat the truth. The pictures from the Gasparilla Half-Marathon in February of 2014 are all hideous. I either look angry, or just fed up. Not a surprise though, because during that race I was feeling tired and burned out. Plus, they must have played "Eye of the Tiger" in four different places—enough with that song!

Despite some of the most unflattering shots ever, it's fun to view the photos online and think back to how the temperature was, the song I heard at mile ten, and remembering the sign that says "worst parade ever." I like the finish line photos too, when there is a clear one to choose. But the hands-down, best race photo ever? Space Coast Marathon, November 2011. This is a great, small race, with about one thousand runners, a beautiful course, a surprising amount of crowd support, and a fantastic post-race meal consisting of breakfast on one side of a grassy park, and pizza on the other.

I was less than a mile from the finish, and out in the street Audrey and Ethan brought cups of Gatorade to me, cheered me on, and wanted me to stop and chat. David took the picture of me taking the cups from the kids while mid-stride, which of course made it into the scrapbooks, and is forever etched in my memory.

Chapter 5
Sometimes There
Is an "I" in Team

Even if you have a lot of family nearby or a huge support group of friends, the bulk of responsibility often is with the mom. There are exceptions, of course, as everyone's situation is different. Just a few weeks before my first child would be born, I was beginning to freak out a little. We did not have any family in town and I had already quit my job at this point, and on a drive home one night, I looked at David and said, "I'm a little nervous."

"About what?" he asked, having no clue that he was about to witness a mini meltdown.

"Well, it's all happening so fast. I mean, I am glad, and I'm excited to meet the baby and be a mom, but I'm nervous about who I'm supposed to *be* now. What am I going to *do*??"

I started delivering newspapers when I was eleven years old. I babysat, worked in food service, a pool store, retail, you name it. I had always worked, sometimes multiple jobs, and although I admit I was getting a little bored in my career, I was proud of my accomplishments and had trouble envisioning a life without quantifiable production. It was scary to walk away from a world

I knew, and with the first sound of the new baby's cry, my life would forever be changed.

David, the calm one of the two of us, came up with a comforting answer that day and at a stoplight, he turned to look me in the eye and said, "You're going to do great. You're ready. You're going to take good care of the baby, and raise it to be a wonderful person, and that's all that matters."

The moment Audrey was born, life got very busy, and there was no time to spend floundering about the meaning of life. Although, I remember the panic when David left for work and I would be home alone with Audrey for the first full day. My parents had already gone home to Rochester after meeting her, and I was running solo. Oh no, where are my teammates? Did I take a wrong turn in the woods somewhere?

What was surprising is that I could use a lot of my professional, transferrable skills, and use them right away. One of which was joining a mom's group. Stay-at-home-mom was almost a misnomer because we were never home! We went to playgrounds, playdates of all sorts, we *lived* at the library, and never missed the weekly group story time. My friends and I found so many free or very inexpensive activities for kids, and it was wonderful to have a little posse. I didn't feel so alone.

As much as we loved these outings with our kids, one thing we all agreed on was getting home in time for a real nap—for the kids that is. If one of these kids fell asleep on the car ride home for even five minutes, that was it. *For the day.* That wouldn't work at all. That precious little "free time" to get a few things done around the house, start dinner prep, return phone calls or emails was huge. Some independence was absolutely crucial with David having a lot of work travel and no family in town. I was the CEO, the nurse, the janitor, and the activities coordinator. I stayed fairly organized and put those transferrable skills to use.

Once the afternoon nap was complete, we spent the later

part of the day reading, coloring, or dancing. Sometimes we took a short walk to gather where she made it her mission to look for sticks and also began her love of sidewalk chalk in the driveway. We had a blast. The preschool years with both of my kids were magnificent, and I knew I was lucky to have easy, healthy babies. They rarely cried, and were adaptable, social, and loved being outside. I managed the schedule and the house, and the time flew. I wish I had known then how easy it was and how much harder it was going to get.

The icing on the cake was when Audrey was big enough to take some spins in the jogging stroller. I could run us two miles to a playground, hang out for a while on the slides and swings, and then run us home. It was perfect—mom and runner at once. How about that? You can have your freedom and push it around with you too. The jogging stroller may be one of the best pieces of baby gear I ever owned, simply because it did provide that freedom to run without having to pay a babysitter, which of course I have done many times since then, because they got too big for the stroller and wouldn't have tolerated more than six miles anyway.

Life has a fine sense of humor though, because as Audrey started kindergarten and Ethan started a three-morning per week preschool program, that very same identity crisis set in again! Can you believe it?? I was used to my role, proud of it, even when in social groups filled with professional career moms, I never apologized for being "just" a stay-at-home mom. My current job was now being outsourced. No more story time, forget picnics at the park. I actually cried when we said goodbye to Miss Patty, the librarian, at the end of that summer. Our group had been a fixture at her story time since Audrey was a month old. We hugged as I said, "Thank you so much for being such a big part of the kids' childhood. This has meant so much to me."

My team was shrinking, it was all changing, and there was

nothing I could do about it. I was no longer CEO of our schedule because school set the calendar. The kids of the mom's group were all going to different pre-schools, and schedules would be different. When you make the decision to be Mom, your role changes with the changing needs of the family, and that can be tricky without an anchor. And even though I was sad to say goodbye to those library days, Ginny and I would start training in mid-September for the 2010 Disney Marathon while the kids were in preschool. Training separately, but together.

As I started training for my second marathon, I took my faithful running by the hand and off we went. I dusted off that training log from seven years ago, found the colorful markers, re-read Hal Higdon's *Marathon,* and made all the necessary mileage notes on the calendar for the eighteen weeks of training. I even bought a copy of *Marathon* for Ginny, to commemorate the occasion. I didn't realize at first what great timing this was to do another marathon. I ran before David left for work and he was very generous with Saturday mornings, skipping a lot of golf or changing his times, so I could get my long runs in. Ginny and I called each other and compared notes about our increasingly long runs, how many burrs we had to pick out of our socks, and which gas station had the most toilet paper and best selection of sports drinks. It was as awesome, and as perfect as running can be.

Our families stayed the night before the marathon at a Disney hotel, and our husbands and kids toasted us over plates of penne the night before our big race. We saw each other only once during the race, near mile eighteen. We agreed at the start of this crazy idea that we would let each other run her own race, no strings attached. For one thing, she *had* to. It was her first and I knew she had to see that she could do it. It was not the time for me to go ask for a running buddy. Plus, I had run this race seven years prior, and I wanted to see if I could cut a few minutes off my time. At the finish line, I was greeted by my good sport of a husband and freezing, adorable children, and there it was again. The tears, the joy, the pounding heart, the cheering, and the triumphant feeling of my chest bursting open as I crossed the finish line. I remembered this, I knew this feeling, it was magical. But the one thing that made it a little different was the thing that made it even more special. I wasn't alone. My family and running were connected, and I couldn't imagine one without the other. Finishing a marathon is great, but seeing the faces of your family at the finish line puts the exclamation point on the accomplishment, because receiving their love is much greater than receiving any medal. My little teammates are growing up.

Running has been a constant during these transitions because it's something that is just mine, but easily shared with others for connection. It's something I can control and have when I need it, and is woven throughout all the other chapters of my life. And as the kids get older, I will have increasing amounts of "free-time." However, the time often gets easily filled with volunteering at school, Bible study, house projects, and errands. Sometimes I think about going back to work but the three people I love the most rarely remember to turn off lights or shut doors. They are not ready to be weaned yet. "Honey, where do we keep the peanut butter? Have you seen my tennis racket? What's our address?" This is a good course for me right now, because it's mostly flat, with only a few challenging hills, and really cute spectators.

I sometimes struggle with the self-imposed guilt trip of thinking how self-indulgent running, particularly training for long races, can be. I talked with one mom who plainly stated that her husband "wouldn't support it." *Ouch.* On the one hand, the non-supportive husband has a point. It takes a lot of time. A fifteen-mile run can take around three hours, which is enough for a part-time job. Ideally, I'd like to try to run one marathon each year for as many years as I can, and only one, partly because of how much time the training takes, so even that will depend on what else is going on. On the other hand, as my kids get older, there are benefits. They see their mom taking care of her health, reaching goals, and including them on trips to the big races. They have cheered on other runners and have asked to start running with me once in a while. I find this especially important for all of our daughters. When starting to run, we are told not to do "too-much too-soon," but our culture is so sadly the opposite. Our kids' childhoods are getting swallowed bit by bit, as evidenced in kids' clothing, popular music, and all sorts of media outlets. My daughter gets to see that I can dress up for meetings at school and be equally as comfortable in my running gear. We running moms help solidify the notion that our girls can think for themselves, instead of solely and blindly being led by whatever current culture says is cool. So, for now, my bib still reads, "Corral M" for Mom.

Career moms should get double the medals, like the Goofy Challenge at Disney where runners run a half-marathon on Saturday and a full marathon on Sunday, except you're doing both all in one day instead of two separate days. I have no idea how late you stay up catching up with laundry, permission slips, or work from the office. But you also set the example that our kids can wear many hats at once and still have time to fit in some mileage.

I was in the kids' dentist office waiting room and noticed a magazine called *Working Mother*, so out of curiosity, I picked it up to see what topics the working moms read about. I was surprised that the bulk of it was like any other parenting magazine, complete with recipes, healthy lifestyle tips, party planning, gift ideas, and crafts. The biggest difference was this section highlighting women of the year. I definitely felt lazy after reading about women with four kids who search for disease cures. Some were pioneering fair work hours for working moms in their corporations, some were inventors, and I was very impressed by their stories. I doubt I'll ever cure a disease, but I feel good that every seemingly insignificant job I do is supporting my family in the pursuit of their dreams. Like I said, it was very strange for me not to work, but sometimes the head coach has to skip a few of her own races so that she can build others up for theirs, and I'm grateful for the little team that formed around me.

Chapter 6
Pass the Pasta, it's
Time to Carb-Load

There are so many sources and experts available for nutritional advice—you can't take out your garbage without hearing about the latest "it" nutrition trend. Kale is quite the popular guy these days. I confess to being a quinoa nut. Other than what I read in health magazines and books, I have no professional nutritional training, but if you want to hear some funny food stories, and how I have become a more mindful eater, pull up a chair. But, please don't judge me if I steal a few fries from one of the kids' plates.

I love to bake. I think it's so cool that flour, butter, sugar, and eggs can come out of the oven in so many different forms. It's culinary magic and mystery. Growing up, nothing said "special occasion" like the platters of Italian cookies from our favorite bakery, piled up in tiers like a cake, aptly named "Cookie Cake." The layers of butter cookies with pastel icing, and the almond paste swirls with one red maraschino cherry told the world, "Something exciting is happening today!"

I bake ten kinds of cookies at Christmas. For a family of four, that sounds almost gross, but there is a method to the distribution. We have our own supply, but I give away many of them to teachers, friends, and neighbors. Also, David's family comes to stay with us for New Year's each year, and I save a ton for that week. So, the *entire* gingerbread family does not take up residence in my thighs, just a few of the distant gingerbread cousins.

Some cookies are tradition, made each year for a reason. Each family member has their personal favorite, and I like to have a few experiments each year. I traipse through December chanting, "I never met a cookie I didn't like." Runners are healthy eaters and have a healthy lifestyle overall, so we also have the luxury of knowing that a few extra cookies here and there aren't going to show up *here* and *there*.

This love of baking was really born out of Christmas Eve memories. After a very traditional Polish meal including things like sausages, sauerkraut, stuffed cabbage rolls, and rye bread, we all looked forward to the platters of cookies brought into my aunt's dining room. With Christmas lights aglow, and Clark Griswold from Christmas Vacation overheard from the family room, we all crowded around that table, spinning the trays to see which one to eat first. My aunt and my grandmother did all of the baking. I am not even sure how many they made, but what I do remember is being there for visits in the weeks prior to Christmas, and me and my cousins sneaking Italian meatball cookies from the basement fridge and freezer, where they stored them until the big day.

I have an Italian cookbook from Rochester, New York with all of these old, traditional recipes, and the ones for meatball cookies, which are basically a spiced, chocolate ball, say things like, "makes a lot," or "makes approximately 225 to 250 cookies." My aunt and grandma would certainly not miss a handful.

Eating all those cookies with the butter, sprinkles, and spices was not only delicious, but it was part of our holiday tradition. When I think of Christmas Eve, one of the memories is of my aunt's house, packed with noisy relatives and a ton of us kids bouncing off the walls, and I knew that someday I would create these moments for my own family. Unfortunately, I was a horrible baker at first, and for many years to follow, but I kept at it.

I attempted baking after college, and my first homemade sugar cookies were like dried up cardboard that crumbled in your hand. The next year, they didn't crumble, but they could almost break teeth. I made a cake for one of David's birthdays and brought it to his parent's house for a party. Because everyone was so nice and knew I tried so hard, they all smiled politely and ate it, but it was a dry, dense, flavorless boulder. The frosting was pretty, though. So even though the first few miles—*and cookies*—are tough, and progress is slow, we have to keep trying.

Because runners love autumn so much, and we live far away from our extended families, Thanksgiving was something else I wanted to master. The kids needed to learn that there really are four different seasons, and the foods of fall are very special. I go out of my way to decorate the house with autumn and harvest décor, so they have a tiny peek at the uniqueness of that season. I have the meal down to a science now, but I make a "Practice Thanksgiving" menu once or twice a year before the *Super Bowl of Cooking,* as I like to call it, just to be sure and possibly try out an interesting new side dish. Our holiday traditions are just as important as our race-day rituals, and I am the Thanksgiving Day Head Coach of Cooking in our home. I start the day by repeatedly asking, "Why is gravy sooo good? Come on. Who knows?" The kids generally roll their eyes and wait for the Macy's Thanksgiving Day Parade to start while playing backgammon with Daddy. I always add, "Maybe this is the year I should try out for the Rockettes. What do you think, honey?"

Traditionally, there are insane amounts of butter, lots of white bread in the stuffing, and three kinds of pies. And since I am a fan of tradition, yes, I'll have another heap of stuffing, it only comes once a year. Using sidewalk chalk on the driveway in bright, gigantic letters, I write "I LOVE STUFFING!" just in case the neighbors wanted to be sure. The things our moms and grandmothers cooked for special occasions are part of our family memories. I vow that I will never bother reading any recipes that claim to have "healthy" holiday favorites. Who wants to look back and say, "We never had pie on Thanksgiving because mom said it wasn't good for you." We want to look back, smell the celery cooking down, softening in the pot, and taste the stolen spoonfuls of mashed potatoes. We'll play our family football game, go for a walk, and have a salad tomorrow.

In addition to their culinary holiday memories, I am also teaching my kids the basic nutritional information that I didn't have when I was their age. In my Polish-Italian heritage, we ate piles of pasta, meat and potato dishes, and pizza. The only fish we ever ate was usually on Fridays during Lent. And it was deep-fried. Literally called "fish-fry." In Rochester, there is a culinary wonder known as the Trash Plate. Some restaurants call it the Garbage Plate. For those of you unfamiliar with this, you choose between hot dogs or cheeseburgers, and then two— yes, I said two—of your chosen item are accompanied by a pile of baked beans, macaroni salad, potato salad, and possibly some sort of meat-based hot sauce or gravy. We had no idea this was a gut bomb. All we knew was that it was a fun time out at a local legend with your friends, and it was *very* yummy.

Things were just as wonderfully caloric in Buffalo. At any social event there, you can count on two things: Pizza and Wings. It's not a party unless these two main attractions are in attendance. My mother-in-law called to tell us about a baby shower she attended, and when I asked her the basic questions of where it was, who was there, and what they served, sure enough, her answer to that last one included pizza and wings. At these parties there are other things to nibble on, such as mayo-clad potato salad, taco dip, and bread dip. I'm sure at some point I would have figured out this nutritional labyrinth, but honestly, I had no idea what I was doing to myself for many years. I made my own bad choices.

David and I were headed out to a Valentine's Day dinner dance in the late 1990's, and only hours before the dinner, I had to go buy a new dress because I was not able to zip any of my others. *Ouch*. I knew I was in trouble and had to make some changes. I think I started running again the following week, and since I was in my twenties with youth on my side, I could see a big improvement in a very short time. Little did I know, that wouldn't always be the case. I simply didn't have any comprehension of a key factor in maintaining a healthy weight: *Calorie density*. "It's just a cup of broccoli cheese soup. How bad can that be?" I'm tall and could "hide" ten extra pounds in my huge wool sweaters of denial, but that couldn't go on forever.

Growing up with those terrifying eating habits meant that, even though I was in track and cross-country, I was far from the skinniest girl in a singlet. I wasn't obese by any means, but being tall, I often felt a bit bigger than the other runners to begin with. When we started wearing running tights, it was cool if your tights were a bit baggy because that meant you looked even more like a "real runner."

I am so grateful that we come in all shapes and sizes these days. Despite the fact that I don't remember anyone referring to me as heavy or overweight, I automatically compared myself and knew I wasn't as thin as the other girls. What a dumb thing to do to myself. Even at this age, and in far better shape than I expected to be, there are occasions when I still feel fat even though I know I'm not. "Does my butt look big? Does it??" Running is the antidote for my mind to remember that I am not fat and have no reason to even think about it. One run of four miles won't take an inch off my belly, but it does put the inner critic in a time-out. And after enough time-outs, the inner critic

Sheila Scott

learns that if she doesn't have something nice to say, she won't say anything at all.

My grandmother, however, was way ahead of her time, and a great example of a health-conscious cook. She was Italian, married to my Polish grandfather, and could really cook anything. She always served a small salad before dinner, and did things like faux fry before that term was even invented. On Fridays, she and my aunt cleaned the house and made home-made chicken soup with pastina for lunch. *Mmmmm.* She cooked everything but always went very easy on salt, fat, and portions. She could also take a look through the fridge and pantry, and transform the oddest ingredients into one of the best meals ever, like the show *Chopped,* but in the 1980's. I like to think I inherited that skill from her because some of my best dinners have been the ones I just can't seem to replicate.

After many years of losing and gaining the same five to ten pounds, I had the rock-bottom moment to get serious about nutrition. Audrey was about five months old. My mother came to visit, and when she returned home, she sent back a cheerful set of pictures from her trip. The one that was the turning point was a side view of me holding my precious little girl, and I looked so full, just fluffy and puffy. This was during the South Beach Diet craze, so a few days later, I bought a copy of the book. Before you start reminding me that runners need carbs, I know, but at that time, I wasn't running at all. This diet was all in favor of the complex carbs though, like vegetables and beans, which contain a lot of good carbs. It was also very educational about calories, sugar, fiber, protein, and calorie density. I knew a little about healthy food choices, but this was the first time I felt like I was starting to really understand what foods did for us, both good and bad. I followed the plan to the letter and started doing workout videos, which are very effective if you stick with them. I even continue to use them for cross-training.

The weight came off. I pushed the baby jogger with Audrey

enjoying the ride in the fresh air, and I never looked back. I finally knew what to do each day to maintain a healthy weight and still be able to enjoy cooking and eating. Having all this new information about basic nutrition, I changed my own palate and recipes, and was much better prepared to help my kids' eating habits develop in a more healthful way, as opposed to thinking turkey bacon subs with mayo were fine. Turkey's healthy, right??

Fortunately, David is a great person to cook for. He's always willing to at least *try* some new experiment. But he too grew up in that food culture of fried and fat, so I am grateful that he has been willing to go along with whatever I want to make for dinner. We both are huge fans of vegetables, and two of my favorite things to make are clean-out-the-fridge salads and clean-out-the-fridge soups. Budget friendly, nutritious, and easy. When you cook at home you can ease up on salt, fat, and sugar. I avoid fried foods and swap out white breads and pastas, to whole wheat sometimes. I try not to be obsessive about it, just guide them into making good choices as they grow.

"Mom, what are we having for dinner?" every mother in America is asked at least once in the afternoon. If my answer is "spaghetti and meatballs," or "chicken tacos," or the most wonderful, "I think we'll have breakfast for dinner and keep it simple since Daddy is travelling tonight," I can count on cheers of joy, balloons falling from the ceiling, and possibly even juggling clowns passing through the house. If my answer is one of the things they are still on the fence about like faux-fried panko-crusted cod, I generally reply with, "I'm not sure yet. I'm still checking my e-mails. Why don't you see if anyone is outside to play with?"

Cooking at home certainly makes it easier to expose the kids to things other than the choices on a kid's menu, which is normally the tired-out chicken tenders, mac & cheese, or a cheeseburger. But it does take some finesse, and I can't let them see me sweat when I introduce something new. I try to avoid eye contact when I serve them a spoonful of barley and vegetable salad on the side of their main dish. A positive we have already seen is that Audrey is not a fan of chain restaurants, because no matter what she gets it's usually "too salty." A ten-year-old gets it.

Another reward to cooking meals most nights is being able to wander through the Wonderful World of Leftovers the next day. Aahhhh. I love being out for a run, finishing up errands, and coming home to good food that is already made, or at least mostly made. I purposely make extra vegetables at dinner so I have them ready for my lunch the next day. Add some more salad, sliced turkey, or a tuna packet and a pita, and done. Just shaved ten minutes off my lunch PR time.

Of course, they never complain about anything being too sweet. We all love our sweets in this house, but in moderation, not like Willy Wonka's factory is going out of business. David and I keep a stash of chocolates for our own evening treats, and the kids have their own little bowls so they can have something small after school. I think they have a good understanding of what's a *small-amount* kind of food, and what's a *whenever* food, like fruit or yogurt. If I can help them be able to stop at a reasonable portion, they will have this skill for their lifetimes. I had to develop that skill on my own—it was all too easy to inhale a sleeve of Thin Mints without batting an eye. Now I know better, well, I still might take down a sleeve after a ten-miler, since the sleeves are much shorter than they used to be.

When Audrey rode in the stroller, I packed snacks like peas and soft cooked carrots to put on the stroller tray. That always got a mixed bag of reactions, from the "What a good mom!" to the "What are you doing to that poor kid?" But I was very deliberate about exposing the kids to all fruits and vegetables as much as possible.

Now at eight and ten, there isn't a fruit they won't eat. Well, except one. Ethan's favorite is strawberries, and coincidentally, Audrey doesn't "like" her little brother's favorite. Hmmmm, sounds suspicious. They love asparagus, salads, and even brussels sprouts. We need to work on tomatoes and beets. In the crusade of broadening their young palates, I pay them for trying a new food. "If you take one normal person bite, you can have twenty-five cents. If you like it and try more, then you can have fifty cents."

Wondering what the catch is, they ask, "What if I don't like it?"

"That's okay, you can still have the twenty-five for giving it a try." I think it's a genius idea, and people have been paid for far worse things than taking a bite of a grilled vegetable panini. They should be grateful! I had no idea as a kid that avocado was something other than a paint color for kitchens. The great part is, they are occasionally finding new things they like, which makes the dinner menus a lot easier to plan.

The past several summers, I have attempted growing some of our own vegetables in large containers. Ethan absolutely loves to plant flowers in the yard, tomato plants in pots, and green bean seeds just beneath the surface of the soil. Every day, he goes out to see if there is any progress. Like running, you don't see dramatic changes quickly. In fact, you may experience set-backs, like realizing bees are an important factor to some vegetable plants and needing to start over, this time *outside* the screened-in patio. But if you keep at it, the strong little buds will appear, and soon they take off vibrantly. Although, some years there is just too much rain, and no matter how hard I try, the plants just drown and we realize we have to wait until next season. That's always a sad thing. Both kids love picking the vegetables once they are ripe, and since they had a hand in the reaping and sowing, they are usually eager to have these home-grown vegetables on their dinner plate. Or, at the very least willing to take one bite for a shiny quarter.

We also seek out small farms that allow people to come in and pick their own produce. Our favorite is a blueberry farm near our house, so we go a little crazy each year, coming home with too many to eat. We usually make a pie and give bags away to their teachers. Mostly, I want them to see how special it is to know where food comes from and be able to collect it ourselves sometimes.

Even though they fit the description of "good eaters," they too have their funny quirks, and things they won't touch. Audrey stopped loving milk a long time ago, so we allow some strawberry powder, or those fun flavored milk straws to get it down. She loves this one kind of decaffeinated blueberry tea in the morning. Ethan's favorite thing in the world is macaroni and cheese. He has a ranking system in place of all of his favorites. There is one restaurant in particular with the best macaroni and cheese. It's like alfredo sauce, and he needs a pile of napkins to get through a bowl of it because the sauce is so gooey and drippy. Mommy and Daddy sometimes *help* him finish it.

Let's all confess, most runners agree, we have our own silly eating rules for race day, as well as the night before. Remember: *Nothing New On Race Day.* Yet, I don't over-think dinner before a marathon, and don't purposely hunt down pasta.

The night before the Space Coast Marathon in 2011, we were unfamiliar with the town, it was getting late, and all we found was a family sports pub. Even there, I managed to order a chicken and rice dish, and that was fine. Of course, when in Chicago, we were all interested in enjoying some deep-dish pizza. David had some colleagues there and one family met us at Giordano's. The place was packed with eaters donning running shoes, all with the same goal of topping off their glycogen stores. The kids loved all the stretchy cheese, and I felt entitled to enjoy an ambitious amount that night.

The pre-race dinner is about more than just the carbs. It's a time to gather my thoughts, think about the next morning, and give gratitude to my family for going along with these races. Having friends with us in Chicago and that one race in Disney turned out to be really special, memorable nights of laughter and closeness—the calm before the calf strain.

In the morning, I like one or two bagels from the packaged bread aisle, and one or two of the individual sized peanut butter containers. I take it easy on the water so I can decrease or eliminate the need to stop for a potty break mid-race. I make a hotel-room coffee to try and "answer nature's call" before I leave the lit, heated, private, toilet-paper-stocked hotel. After all, at 5:30 a.m., the only thing worse than a porta-potty, is a *dark* porta-potty. Plus, we have all been through trial and error on our preferred method of energy supply mid-race. Some flavors are terrifying, others are ok, and some burn my insides.

Armed with nutritional expertise, the toughest part is, of course, making my way through the grocery stores. Sometimes...with *Them*. It's so much easier to do the grocery shopping on my own. I can read labels carefully, look through the coupons, and focus on the list. When the kids are with me, it starts with Ethan looking for spare change by belly-crawling on the floor in front of the soft-drink machines by the shopping carts. He always finds money, ranging from a single penny to as much as eighty cents.

Working through the produce section, I send one to get a bag of spinach, and the other to pick out a container of blueberries, and we move smoothly along. A few episodes of back-talk occur near the bakery over cookies, and another mom will give me a knowing smile of, "I get it, hang in there, sister!" I'll make a comment along the lines of, "They know everything at this age, don't they?" Both of us moms give a slight chuckle.

I realize that Audrey is officially at the age of being embarrassed by me. The tables have turned. Now, instead of just me being embarrassed by them, I have gained the power to cause

Sheila Scott

the same undeserved humiliation that I have suffered with for years. Insert evil, maniacal laugh.

On a recent trip to the store, she said to me, "I wish that as soon as everyone came into the store, none of their ears worked."

"Why is that, honey?" I smirked, knowing where this was headed.

"Because, they don't need to hear everything I say and make some cutesy comment about it."

"Oh, well don't worry about it. They are just being friendly," I reassured.

This episode passed quickly when she spied the caramel rice cakes and forgot all about the other shoppers. We got through the rest of the list and a stop to the restroom before making it to the finish, I mean, *checkout* line. Ethan ran over to the copy machine and change-counting machine to look for more money. Then, *I assure you, I have said it every single time while in line for the register.* "Please don't swing on the bar!" Sadly, they still swung on the bar that separates the checkout lanes. I was trying, really, I was. Those forty-five minutes were a nutrition-hunting warrior dash, well, more like a zombie run.

Chapter 7
Ouch! I Have a Boo-Boo!

Pain, injuries, and illness go hand in hand, both in running and motherhood, and being both a runner, and a mother gives us a higher threshold for pain tolerance. And how many of you have a preferred parking space at the emergency room lot?

Ethan was, and often still is, always finding himself in physical pain. When he was about a year old, he was climbing up the double oven, which caused the door to open, so he fell backward to the hard floor, hitting his head and scraping off a lot of skin from his toe. This, we were able to handle at home with plenty of ice and gauze. Ethan's first hospital visit was when he was about a year and a half. I was in the kitchen making dinner and watched him lean over a small side table in the family room, reaching for his sippy cup, and his fall caused a slice in his earlobe. It's amazing that you can *see* a fall as it's happening, and be totally helpless because three feet might as well be a mile. I grabbed the kids and the diaper bag, turned off the stove, and off we went for stitches.

He was a little more than two for his next visit, while I was on a weekend trip to New York City with two friends from college. I made the morning phone call on Saturday, and the kids were fine. They had a good breakfast, and they were on their way to one of our favorite parks on a perfect February day in Florida. As David put Ethan in the swing, he noticed a golf ball-sized lump on the side of his neck. He immediately drove them to the emergency room, where the doctors discovered he had an abscess, caused most likely by an undiscovered ear infection. It's freezing in February in New York, so my flip-phone was tucked in a purse, which was tucked in a coat, and I didn't hear it all day. We were bustling around from museums to stores and never even went back to the hotel before dinner. But, when I took the phone out of my coat and purse to call at dinnertime and saw that he had called at least ten times, I knew something was up. I learned of the anesthesia and surgery to remove the abscess. But like a caged-up tiger, I was not able to get a flight home that night. My heart was broken, and I felt useless.

I hopped on a very early flight the next morning, and when I finally got to the hospital via cab from the airport, Ethan looked so small, lying in that big bed with all the tubes attached to him. I hesitated by the door with my hands over my mouth, until the doctor said, "It's okay, you can go hug him." I went to his bedside and he backed away from me a little. I cried because I thought he, at two years old, was mad at me for not being there, or had already forgotten who I was after only two nights. I can't believe I wasn't there for him. It makes me sad to this day. I felt as helpless as I ever had in my life. David, though, was "the man." He managed everything beautifully, even though he was a mess having to see his little man get wheeled down the hall to surgery, with no one there to support him. He called some friends, who picked up Audrey and took care of her, so he was truly alone in that experience. Suffice it to say, I was not in a huge hurry to go away again any time soon.

My friendships are very important to me, but when you are

away from a child and helpless to get there when they need you, it gives you a new perspective.

But, let's back this story up just a week, to the night before Super Bowl XLIII, which took place here in Tampa. I was lucky enough to be attending with David the next day, my first and probably only Super Bowl. Overnight Saturday, Ethan kept waking up and cried all night long. I took him for a car ride at 2:00 a.m., then we brought him into bed with us and turned on Blue's Clues, but nothing calmed him back to sleep. He had no symptoms of anything, no fever, and no stuffiness, so this just didn't make any sense, especially since he never did this before. We must have fallen asleep around 4:00 a.m. and he was absolutely fine the next day, as though the night before never happened. I even have pictures of us at a playground during that day, before we left the kids with a sitter to go to the game. The sitter said he was fine that night, perfectly normal, and he was healthy the entire following week.

But since this was going to be only my second time away from the house by myself, I was a bit nervous anyway. I remember trying to come up with reasons for how I could back out of this trip because it was such a strong, bad feeling in the pit of my stomach, but of course it made no sense at the time. On the way to the airport at 5:00 a.m., there was an enormous traffic accident just before our exit to the airport. My friend and I just sat on the highway for an unbelievable amount of time, which simply never happened at this time of day. We barely made our flight. We ran to the gate with our shoes still in our hands from the security line. Sometimes, we need to listen to our instincts. Moms just *know*.

Ethan's next mishap didn't require a trip to the emergency room, but it was still exciting. We were visiting David's parents up north, about to leave the house to get to the airport. He was running through the kitchen and tripped on a chair leg. He bit his lip so hard that it sliced and bled like crazy. We finally got it to stop and still made the flight. His one top tooth, however, remained gray ever since the collision from the fall. It never bothered any of us. It was just a good story, and since we had been on the Tooth Fairy's regular route, it didn't take long for that baby tooth to be replaced.

Audrey has had few injuries or illnesses, but when she was at her six-week check-up, our very observant pediatrician noticed that she had right *torticollis*, which is a fancy way of saying the muscles on one side of her neck were tight and pulling her head down toward the side. I had no idea. I just figured she had a typical floppy baby neck. He kept looking at her, studying her neck intently. He sent her in for some x-rays, where I became a frantic mess. Remember how tiny a six-week-old baby is? They are really, *really* small. They used wide Velcro straps to tie her to a wood plank that looked fresh out of the hardware store, and it was tilted at approximately a forty-five-degree angle. She looked like a child's doll. My special assignment was to hold a strip of fabric under her chin and pull her head back straight. She cried and cried with all her might. Her face turned red, and it was a horrible thing to see and participate in. These are the heart-wrenching moments of, "I know this is awful, but we have to do this to take care of you."

Upon reviewing the x-rays, the pediatrician's suspicions were correct and we had to take her to a pediatric physical therapist. This individual taught us stretching exercises to do with her several times a day. One of which was to lay her on her back, turn her face to the side with the flat palm of our hand, and hold it there for counts of ten. I was basically pinning her down and squishing her face against the carpet with my hands —lovely. We also had to tilt her head down to her shoulder to stretch out these shortened muscles. I cried for at least the first week of doing this, because she was clearly uncomfortable. Fortunately, it was only a three-month period and she got used to it very quickly. Soon, she didn't cry, and neither did I, and her muscles lengthened out normally. Take it from a six-week-old baby, stretching is important for our muscles.

Then, there are the run of the mill ear infections that keep them banned from swimming. It's so hot and sunny, the pool is sparkling, and they have to wait until the infection clears up. A whole pack of our friends were sick with sinus infections one summer, after we all went to the same bounce house place, a petri dish of injuries and illnesses. Every mother I know has *at least* one bounce house place horror story. Some kids fall off the tops of the bouncy slides and break legs, some kids get trapped in the obstacle course, unable to breathe. Yet, when the party invitation comes rolling in, we'll head into the minefield once more.

At our house, we go through Band-Aids like water, which I suppose is good because they are very active outside, and skinned knees are just a side effect of a good time. But some are barely a visible scrape, and the Band-Aid is used solely as an emotional healer. The bad cuts are scary, though. I have to pull myself together to be able to handle the yuckier ones. David is ok with blood, so if he's home, he is the expert there.

I always feel terrible when they have what we call, "the barfs." It's so sad to see them in pain and so weak. That's when time stands still. Nothing gets done because I physically leave their side only when absolutely necessary, or David can take my seat so I can shower. David relocates to the guest room so I can keep the sickie in bed with me to help them during the night.

Moms get injuries even before the baby arrives, probably to get us used to medical treatment and pain. After the completion of my first marathon, we agreed it was time to "start trying" to have a baby. And like training for a race, I did everything I could to set myself up for a good run. I met with the doctor and jumped off the cliff, I mean, went off the pill. I took the fancy vitamins and stared longingly at the glasses of wine being enjoyed by my friends and family. Miraculously, it happened. I saw the result as clear as day on the little test, and was just over the moon with excitement. To tell David the good news, I ordered a Buffalo Bills bib and bottle for him to unwrap. After work, I greeted him in the kitchen with the package wrapped in plain white paper. We see our husbands cry so little during our lives, but as the light bulb went on, realizing what these things were and what they meant, that was one of the few times he let the tears flow. We were having a baby.

From that moment on, I was barely allowed to move, forbidden from yard work, prohibited from lifting heavy loads of laundry. I patiently waited for him to carry in the heavy jugs of water from the grocery store. I adored the adoring, and allowed him his mother-hen activities because it made him feel important and protective. We told everyone the good news right away, which you're really not supposed to do, but we couldn't keep it a secret. We considered renting out billboard space.

Before I knew it, it was time for the first listening of the heartbeat appointment, which we treated like the most anticipated concert of the year that we had VIP tickets for. David met me at the doctor's office and he sat right by my side as my doctor slid the little gadget across my slimy abdomen. I had been going to her for years and was very comfortable with her.

Minutes passed like hours, our brows furrowed, and my doctor said, "Hmm." Generally speaking, in the medical world "hmm" is about the worst thing you can hear, and usually indicates impending doom.

"Well, Sheila, we'll have to do an internal ultrasound, because we aren't getting the heartbeat this way. Don't worry, we have to do this sometimes if the baby is in a strange position," she calmly told us.

Like a drawstring, my throat tightened and the veins in my forehead protruded. "Oh, okay." I was then directed to change into the "zero modesty gown," and led to another room with dim lighting and a fancy white ultrasound machine.

The technician started by saying, "These tests, we are not able to read to the patients. I have to give the pictures to the doctor, and she will discuss what she finds with you in her office."

"Okay," I whispered and laid there quietly.

"I have taken all the pictures I need, you can go get dressed, and the doctor will see you shortly." She directed me out to where David was waiting, and I slipped into another room to change. Dressed, I sat down next to him in those hideous mauve colored chairs. Soon, my doctor called us into her office.

"This is the worst part of my job. I'm sorry to tell you that there was no heartbeat; you've had a miscarriage. At this point, you have two choices. You can let the rest of the process happen naturally, which I don't recommend because it can be painful and traumatic, or we can set you up for a procedure in the morning."

All I could do was nod at that point, because I felt like I was being choked, and all the air had left my body. My chest was crushed flat.

"I can set up the appointment time right now. You'll go to the Women's Hospital, where another doctor from our practice will perform the surgery," she softly instructed.

Tears stung my eyes, I nodded again, David handled the details, and we drove home. Back in the kitchen, where I gave him the Buffalo Bills bib, we cried, sobbed out loud, and held each other. To this day, I have not seen him cry harder than that day at 5:00 p.m. in our kitchen.

Although we told *everyone*, I only told two of my very close friends at work. They, coincidentally, were also pregnant. We realized in conversation one day that we were all thinking about "trying" at about the same time, so it was like a secret club. We zipped around to each other's offices, giggling and comparing notes in hushed voices. I called them to let them know why I wouldn't be in the next day. What was really surprising about the aftermath of that horror, was how many women said, "Yeah, I understand, it happened to me too." I was shocked at the amount. Despite my wanting things to be different and avoid this terrible pain altogether, there was an undeniable comfort from my women friends. Even though I was alone, I certainly didn't feel like it. Having that kind of crowd support helped me through a rough bunch of miles, and helped me keep sight that there would be another race out there for me.

With exceptions, most running injuries are not quite as traumatic as that, but certainly as varied as those of the kids. Sometimes it's just tummy distress. Not a big deal, unless it's at mile twenty-two. Even colds—they say if your cold symptoms are from the neck up, you can still run, neck down and take a few days' rest. Other than some mild muscle pulls and shin splints in high school, I have had only one major running injury. It was sixteen days before what was to be my third marathon. I was happily in the taper, out for an easy but energetic six-miler. At the start of mile six, I felt a sharp pain in my right heel. I slowed down but the pain persisted. I practically limped into my driveway. I wasn't nervous, and simply decided to take a few days off. I had nothing to worry about because I was in the taper—the hard part of training was completed.

I tried running down the driveway a few days later, and ouch! *Ouch!!* A few days later, no better, still a piercing pain that soared up to my brain. I didn't know what the problem was, so I scrambled to the people at the local running store for advice, wrote posts on *Runner's World* forums, and even begged my chiropractor for a miracle. Nothing. A few days before the race, I still couldn't run two steps on my right foot, so I had to cancel the hotel. Devastating. This particular race was run the Sunday after Thanksgiving, so I had to wait until the following week to call for an appointment with an orthopedist. Meanwhile, I saw all over the walls the turkey handprint pictures the kids and I make every year, and that year, I turned all of mine into running turkeys with Space Coast Marathon singlets. How depressing. Even more depressing was the fact that my body and brain were accustomed to a fair and consistent amount of running, so to suddenly stop the IV drip of endorphins and serotonin that running delivered, sent me into mood swings and periods of tears.

"So, what brings you in this morning?" asked the intake nurse at the modern and high-tech university medical center.

"Well, I was training for a marathon that I was supposed to run last Sunday, but for the past two weeks, I haven't been able to run because the impact on my right heel sends shockwaves of intense pain through my body," I tried to explain.

She must not have been a runner, because no dose of sympathy over the missed race was given out, and I wanted someone to say, "I know just how you feel! And we'll gladly pay for next year's registration for you." But she simply went into the typical questions such as, "Does it hurt to walk on it?"

"No, not at all." I thought that must be a good thing that it doesn't hurt when walking, and maybe it wasn't so bad.

She took a few more notes and said, "The doctor will be in to see you shortly."

While I waited, I felt a bit silly being there, thinking, "It's probably nothing. I should have given it more time before wasting these people's time. There are people here who have real medical problems, like senior citizens needing hips replaced from running too many marathons." The doctor came in, was very pleasant, and asked me similar questions as the nurse. He inspected my naked foot, pressed here and there showing where the pain was, and sent me across the hall for x-rays. I climbed four steps up to a platform where they took bottom and side view photos of my foot. A few magazine articles later, I was invited back in to meet with the doctor.

"You have a stress fracture in your calcaneus," he informed me.

"What's a calcaneus?" I thought, and why on earth do they have to embarrass me with the fancy-schmancy medical terms? Piriformis, gluteus minimus, whatever. My butt is sore and I need a tennis ball. Instead, I asked, "So, is something broken?"

After explaining the fracture was in my heel, the x-ray and the medical mumbo jumbo, he added, "You'll need to wear a boot cast and use crutches for six weeks." He rattled it off like he says it fifty times a day. But I was still in shock at hearing it for the first time ever, trying to make sense of this, and nervous about crutches because I'm not super coordinated to begin with.

"Are you sure?" I asked.

He told me he was certain about the diagnosis and assured me that the time will fly, and that this will soon be a faint memory.

"So, when can I run?" I couldn't help but ask while he fitted me for a boot cast, plucked from the rows and rows of them lining the shelves, waiting for their next victim.

"Oh, it will be a while. You want to be sure this heals up properly or you could make it much worse, so no running, and be sure to use the boot and crutches all the time."

"But can I bike?" If I can't have the whole pint of ice cream, can I have half of a frozen yogurt?

Impressively holding back an eye-roll, he replied, "No, it would be too much pressure on your foot right now, you really have to wait to put any weight on that leg." He sounded like he needed to get to his next appointment, and these silly runners drove him crazy after a while. He adjusted the height of my crutches very kindly and told me to come back in a month, to take another x-ray to check on the healing of the heel. He provided me with referrals to physical therapists who could help get muscle function back up to speed and teach me at-home strengthening exercises.

"Okay, I understand. Thank you very much for all your help." I walked out with the moon-boot on my leg and pathetically carried my running shoe that was without purpose for a while.

Wait, it gets better. Audrey was six, Ethan was four, and Christmas was a month away. But runners aren't about to give up any time soon. I still made all of my ten kinds of cookies, decorated my house, and drove the wheel chair scooters through the malls and grocery stores, crashing into plenty of displays. I did a lot of shopping online that year, and hid the boxes while the kids were at school. A little tip if you are ever in this predicament, wear a re-usable grocery bag around your neck. You'll be amazed at what you can carry around the house if you are on crutches. I had the kids carrying stuff all the time for me, especially dinner plates. That was a tricky one, since I couldn't put a plate of food around my neck. I let them play limbo with my crutches and kept smiling.

I cheated a little and walked some, but only when absolutely necessary. I treated the healing process of this ridiculous injury as a job. I knew that if I was a good little patient and did every-thing I was told, that equaled one very important prize, better than the lollipop or sticker the pediatricians gave out. To be able to run again.

At a later follow up appointment, the fracture was indeed healed, but I was surprised since my heel now felt like it was on fire if I was on my feet for a long time. As it turned out, I had plantar fasciitis. *Grrrr.* I tried a few strong anti-inflammatory medications, but one upset my tummy in ways that should not be repeated to any other human being, and the others simply didn't do much. So, I relied on ice, the night splint, and tape for a while. I eventually went to a physical therapist, which was the turning point for the PF. This new BFF of mine was all about the biomechanics of running, and to get the links in the chain stronger, they had me doing things like pulling wet bath towels across the floor using only my toes, while my heel stayed planted on the floor. I picked up marbles with my toes and used stretchy bands to build up muscles in my feet. It all hurt at first, but I have to say that improvement came quickly as a result of all the strengthening. I stuck with it and was back to a little running about four months after the initial injury.

I missed running so much. I was jealous of runners I saw while driving my kids to school, and I thought, "Do they know how lucky they are right now?" I found ways to maintain physical activity using weights on the floor, lots of abdominal routines and shadow boxing. I knew I had to do something or else I'd really go crazy. But with some imagination, and my mental super-power, I knew I could hang on.

My next run-in with the world of medicine came in the spring of 2013, just before school let out for the summer. It was a warm Saturday morning and I had run a little bit, and then spent some time doing weights. The kids were enjoying a relaxed morning of their own, watching their shows, coloring, and just playing with their toys after a late breakfast. I started helping the kids with their homework while David was catching up on bills and paperwork, and waiting for a visit from a friend that was going to help us with some small improvement projects in the house. I was in a room printing some things out for a project that Audrey was working on, and I heard the door-bell ring. As I stood up from a squatting position near the laptop, which I had placed on the floor next to the printer, I made my way toward the front of the house. I suddenly had to hang on to a small table because my vision went blurry, and my entire body started shaking. I really thought my legs were going to give out. I just stood there for a minute, holding myself up and hoping that our guest at the door couldn't see me, because I'm sure I looked strange. I finally made it to the door as though nothing had happened, invited him in, brought him to the kitchen, and went back to the printer. I wasn't nervous, because this was nothing new for me. I was used to that dizzy feeling when getting up because I have fairly low blood pressure, and even when at a regular check-up, the intake nurse would say, "Hmmm, I think I need to read your blood pressure again."

To which I always reply, "It's low, right? It's always low, but go ahead." The dizziness is one of those things I was always aware of.

Unwilling to learn from the first incident, I squatted down to finish printing the pages for Audrey. After a few minutes, David called me to the other room to get my opinion on something. So, I rose up, and as I turned to leave the room, I blacked out completely. I hit my back on a protruding wall corner and fell to the—fortunately for me—carpeted floor. I tried to raise my head and get up, but I was shaking uncontrollably this time, unable to even tell my arms what to do, and I could do nothing but wait it out. This episode was *very* new to me. I had never just passed out like that. After what was probably less than a minute, my body stilled, I could see, and I got back up. I went to talk to them but didn't say a word about what had just happened.

The only other time I sort-of passed out was after a fifteen-mile run on a very sweltering day. When I dropped the kids off at pre-school, I left my car there while I got the run taken care of. I returned in time to get Ethan from his half-day program, and I stretched against a tree in the front yard of the school. I bent down a bit to give the hamstrings some love and then collapsed. My arms got really weak and floppy, and although I was fully conscious and not injured, I couldn't get up right away, which was frightening because of the fire ant piles near me. Fire ant piles are not something a person wants to be laying near. Hoping no one from inside the school saw this, I finally stood back up, and I walked slowly to my car to get water and find shade. I was a little scared by that but chalked it up to mid-day heat, dehydration, and lowering my head too far below my heart too quickly after the run. I never thought about it again.

But this was much more intense than the tree incident, I was a little scared. Shortly after our friend left and I knew the kids were not in hearing range, I went to David and started to tear up. "I have to tell you what just happened to me."

He knew something was wrong. "What's going on?"

I told him the whole story, and he guided me to the couch and gave me some water. We talked a little more and I felt normal the rest of the weekend, except for the headache that wouldn't go away. I called my doctor first thing Monday morning but she was out of town for the next two weeks. Because of the persistent headache, David and I brought the kids to school and went to the emergency room so they could have a look. After the EKG, a quick CAT scan of my head, and recording my blood pressure while laying, sitting, and standing, they said, "Your tests look great, get out of here before you waste any more of our time and dirty any more of our linens." Those weren't their *exact* words, but it was a huge relief. They instructed me to make a follow-up appointment with my doctor so she could make a record of the event.

When I finally did meet with her a few weeks later, under the assumption that this was just a quick informational visit, I found out that if you tell doctors that you passed out and uncontrollably shook, they will send you in for a cardiac work up. The referral sheet listed syncope and giddiness. I thought that was a mistake, and frankly a bit insulting, because why on earth would they consider my giddiness a medical condition? But that was actually how they recorded fainting. I wasn't thrilled to spend my summer going for cardiac tests, but at least the babysitters would earn a few extra dollars for college.

The test I had some fun with was the tilt table test. They evaluate how different positions affect your blood pressure, and the nurses told me that they are essentially trying to get a person to pass out in a controlled environment. For thirty minutes, I stood on a little ledge connected to a table, tilted ever so slightly you could barely tell—imagine how little your airplane seat reclines. The young nurses were a jovial group, and I told them there was no way they would be able to make me pass out because I am all endurance. If, however, they asked me to have a few glasses of cabernet, only then might they possibly claim victory in the "Make Me Pass Out Test." But with only coffee, water, and yogurt in my system, I would prevail that morning. They chatted to fill time, then finally gave up and let me go.

Even the echocardiogram result was excellent. *Apparently, I have the heart of a racehorse.* Despite my willingness to make a few jokes, inside I was very relieved that my heart was intact. I was all too aware of how serious it could have been. A good enough scare can cast doubt, and with my training for Chicago about to begin, I wasn't going to leave it to chance. I wanted the peace of mind that I could go beat up my lower body in the most careful way possible.

After all of that, I was labeled as having orthostatic hypotension, also known as postural hypotension, which simply means that when the blood pools in your lower body, it takes a bit for your blood pressure to supply the required blood to the rest of your body, which can cause the dizziness. The cardiologist made some standard recommendations about staying adequately hydrated, because being dehydrated could put me at risk for dizziness or fainting.

Sheila Scott

I generally drink plenty of water throughout the day, so that was an easy one. A suggestion for safety is to try and get to the floor if I feel dizzy, so as not to risk a dangerous fall. So, if you see me cris-cross applesauce in the cereal aisle, you'll know why. He also suggested taking salt pills during the hot weather runs because I could stand a little more sodium in my system. So, after I sit and read a little with my coffee and I stand up to go back to the kitchen for a second cup, I might get dizzy, see some cool geometric shapes, and have to stand still for a few seconds. The lesson learned was that we need to check this stuff out, even if it's nothing major, take the time and be sure.

My most embarrassing injury was when I crashed into a tree. I was running along a sidewalk and moved into the grass to allow the couple pushing the stroller to have the sidewalk, and ducked under what looked like soft, feather-like leaves sparkling in the morning sun. I thought the leaves would just brush the top of my cap as I ducked a little to run under. The surprise was that behind the pretty leaves, was a tree branch in the shape of a railroad spike and it knocked me backwards on the ground. The people walking and the neighbors all came over to check on me. There was a fairly good-sized head wound and they called an ambulance to be sure I didn't have a concussion. Fortunately, I was not diagnosed with a concussion, just clumsiness.

Even though it can beat us up at times, running is a healing activity in its own way. This was true for me in the summer of 2010, when my uncle passed away quite unexpectedly. We weren't super close in the later years, but I was still close with my aunt, and they participated extensively in my care and upbringing after my parents' divorce. This is my father's sister, and she and my dad's parents lived in my hometown of Rochester, along with my three cousins. Theirs was a home of laughter, with Pasta Wednesday, Pizza Friday, and church every Sunday. All the cousins ran around like animals, and no one shushed us. They let us be kids. We had a good time there, and I will be forever grateful to them for all they did for me. As I travelled to Rochester for the services by myself, I felt the range of emotions: sad, nervous, and reminiscent. As I was packing, I asked my mom about the time schedules for the services, mostly because I wanted to figure out when I could go for a run. I wasn't all that worried about running or logging miles, because I knew that running would worry about me.

Even though running heals, we get a few weird problems as the miles pile up. One area that never seems to completely heal up is our feet. The evidence of our daily dose of equal parts calm, and hard work is often seen in our little buddies on the ground. I have never lost a toenail, but I certainly know the telltale sign of bandages covering a woman's toes. A woman in my Bible study came in after completing the Goofy Challenge at Disney in 2014, with her toes all wrapped up like little burritos. I congratulated her, and we chatted about lower mileage after a big race like that.

I have had some black spots on my nails, and of course the bottoms of my feet are loaded with thick patches of protection from all the miles. Living in a warm state, we have the luxury of wearing cute sandals most of the year, so we try to keep our feet from making people want to gag, but without giving up our much needed callouses. So, I do my own pedicures. I don't trust the girls at the salons to leave enough behind.

While training for the 2010 Disney Marathon, my friend Ginny went in for a quick pedicure, and upon removing her old polish and seeing her completely black toenail, she actually passed out in the pedicure chair. The girls at the salon were scrambling around trying to figure out what to do, but Ginny woke up quickly and was able to tell them to call her husband to pick her up. She was fine, but very much in shock about what was happening to her body as the weeks went on. She battled shin splints off and on, and had to take a chunk of time off training, which was smart, and yet extremely frustrating. She knew she had to get the miles in, but she also knew if the shins didn't heal up, she wouldn't even see the start, much less the finish. The older I get, the more I can relax about taking that time to heal, instead of pushing myself and doing more damage.

The day of my twenty-mile run before the 2010 Disney, I got up as usual, ate a bit, got dressed, put Body Glide and Icy Hot on their respective places, and popped two ibuprofen tablets. *Uh oh.* I thought I'd help ward off any discomfort by starting with some pain relievers. That was wrong, very, very wrong. Less than a mile down the road, my stomach was hurting like a box of hot nails had been dumped into it. I drank some water, and at the two and a half-mile point I stopped at a gas station to get some crackers for the road, thinking that would calm things down. The crackers didn't help at all, so I ran that entire twenty miles with a piercing sharp pain in my stomach. I later found out that putting ibuprofen in a relatively empty tummy was a dangerous thing to do. Most likely, it was bleeding in there and I simply had to wait it out for a few days. Never again. *If you learn only one thing reading this, let it be that you never, ever take pain relievers on an empty stomach.*

The most painful type of illness I face is when David has a cold. I want to know, is there anything worse than a Man Cold? This guy walks around like limbs are falling off mid-stride. My happy husband becomes a bit grumpy when he has a cold. I want to be sympathetic because I am certain he is uncomfortable and unable to sleep well. I try to help him. "Honey, would you like some Nyquil?"

"Yeah, thanks, *cough, cough, sniff, achoo!*"

"Okay, here you go. In fact, here's a little bit more. A little more. One more sip. That should do it!"

Here's a surprise along the course that I didn't see coming. We spend hours and hours caring for our kids' physical and emotional needs day after day. Then, without warning, they knock your socks off and start returning care to you. Years ago, I threw my back out so badly, I could get around only by crawling. Audrey made me "get well" cards and offered to bring me ice packs. Even if I say my tummy is a little off, she offers to bring me water. When we're really sick and really down for the count, the kids seem to know and even fight a little less. If I pinch my neck, Ethan offers to massage it. And that Gatorade at the end of the Space Coast Marathon is a beautiful picture of kids anticipating another's needs and trying to meet them, wanting to help, of seeing pain and trying to support someone in any way they can.

Chapter 8
Consistency, Cross-Training, and Cutting Back

Early in the morning, while it's still dark, I tiptoe to the bathroom to change into my running clothes and plug my contacts in my eyes. I grab my water bottle, which I filled the night before, and slip out the side door noiselessly, so as not to wake any sleeping lions. I take a deep breath on the front porch. *Ahhh, freedom.*

Sunsets get all the fame in Florida, but I will tell you that it's the sunrises that are the real stars of the show. I happily get up early to run, just to be part of nature at this time of day. The humid air has a faint coolness to it for a bit longer, and the smell of wet mulch, orange blossoms, and pine float through the air. The sky brightens to a periwinkle blue, wet leaves sparkle at every turn, and musical trees fill the streets with the chatter of the birds as they make their plans for the day. If I'm lucky enough to have a few clouds in the sky, I watch the progression of colors begin from purple, to blue, to orange, to pink, to yellow, and finally crisp white. Meanwhile, our ancient oaks dripping with airy Spanish moss get to be part of the show, with the light streaming through all the branches and leaves, like you're really seeing sunrays from heaven.

After a soothing, yet invigorating six miles, I walked into cartoons, and cuddled up kids enjoying their Saturday morning of not being in a hurry.

"Who wants a hug??" I threatened them, and heard the squeals of, "Eeeewww, get away, you stink!!" All the while with a twinkle in their eyes.

"Did you guys make your beds?"

"Not yet."

"Did Daddy make your breakfast?"

"No."

"I asked them." David looked up from the paper. "They said they weren't hungry."

"I'm hungry now, Mommy. Can you make me eggs, and raisin toast, and a smoothie, and apples with Biscoff?" Audrey requested, knowing how to work me with her smile and twinkling eyes.

I briefly considered going back out for another six miles as I navigated the Playmobil-covered hallway, realizing I needed coffee. But I cross-trained, I could get back in the race here.

We have parenting books, blogs, websites, and magazines available at our fingertips. Any question we have about crying, blankets, back talk, tricycles, or poop can be answered. For me, I relied heavily on the books. My favorite, as I mentioned, was *Healthy Sleep Habits, Healthy Child.* I had a few friends in playgroups whose babies simply would not nap. They literally tried everything in the book. *Some kids are just not nappers, I suppose.* But I found it to be true that adequate rest seemed to make everything easier, like the first domino in the line.

In that book, and in every other, the underlying theme on every topic was consistency. Offering a new food? Do it consistently ten to twenty times. While potty training, we gave out M&Ms for a successful potty visit. Our bedtime routine was the same thing every night.

Whatever methods you choose to reach a goal, being consistent with them is how you'll make progress.

Even when time is tight, a short run can also be very beneficial to staying consistent and being energizing. I'm surprised after a speedy, thirty-minute run, how much more alert, and happy I feel. Sweaty, I come back apologizing to my family for unkind things I may have said, or forgetting to show gratitude for something nice done for me. I might even have the solution for what to do with all the visiting relatives. A mere thirty minutes has the power to positively transform our bodies and our minds. The world would be a much friendlier place if everyone ran a few miles.

During my lazy fettuccini alfredo period, when we still lived in Buffalo, a friend and I were talking about running, and she drove this point home. She already had two of her now four kids, and this comment she made stuck with me, "Even if you run only one day during a week, run at least that. Don't let a week pass without at least one day of running."

What fantastic advice. It's so easy to get discouraged if we fall off our routine, but even that one day a week counts in some periods of our lives. While this advice is not going to appear in serious training plans, she had a very realistic view that some weeks would be better than others for a few years, but she kept at it. This was an inspiring and encouraging thought. Consistency can come in many forms, from the most days in a row running, to the most years in a row, including the weeks where it was only one day. It really is cumulative.

I can consistently count on the kids bickering over whose turn it is for the Wii, or the swing, or the blue pen, for crying out loud. But I stay the course, teach them how to solve their differences, send them to time out, and eventually, with this regular pattern of response, I can hope that one day, in a galaxy far, far away, the arguing will cease. Well, if not cease, then at least decrease.

Consistent family traditions are also important to me. I want the kids to have great memories when they get older, and feel the comfort and security in what we did every year. Running is most certainly a sport led by tradition. *Runner's World* is loaded with stories of people that run a particular race every year, even if they have to travel far and wide to get there. There was a big to-do at the 2013 Disney Marathon for the people that ran all twenty of them since its inauguration. They received all sorts of special treatment that weekend, but most likely, that wasn't the initial motivation. While some of those that completed all twenty did so purposefully, maybe some did it quite by accident. "Well, if I've done this many..." But, most of the time the motivation is the comfort in the tradition itself, not the accolades.

We had to design our own traditions after Audrey was born. She was three months old at her first Christmas, when we decided we were not participating in winter or holiday airline travel with our new baby. David's parents came to be with us, which made the transition into our own celebrations smoother. The first couple of years, we missed each of our families' Christmas festivities. It would have been easy, had we still lived near them, to piggyback on what was already being done, but living miles away, we cleared new trails for ourselves.

It takes me three to four days to decorate the inside of the house. Of course, you know about the cookies. We also pile into the car and drive around, looking at as many lights as possible, listening only to Christmas music. We watch all the movies, go ice-skating, and to church on Christmas Eve. After scurrying around as quiet as possible, putting presents in place, hoping neither of them will get up to use the bathroom, we let out a breath of relief. "Whew! We did it again! High five, my love!"

As far as Santa is concerned, we have been diligent beyond belief when it comes to this guy. There are notes left a few times during December, and those silly elves, the Elf on The Shelf elves, have really helped enhance the magic and confirm the belief. Our elves have had snowball fights, stolen socks for sleeping bags, been buried in candy wrappers and marshmallows, and for the finale last year, they were flying from the ceiling fan. David and I agree every year, "The day will come when they won't believe, so do it up now and stay the course, so they will have sweet memories." When they have their own families, they might not do things exactly like we did, but we sure led them to the start line.

But no one is perfect, and I'll confess to being a hypocrite in adhering to traditions at any cost. There was this one time when I put my desires before those of my children. Okay, there were probably a few other times, but this was the one that made them take notice and let me know their opinions. So, as much as I love and depend on traditions, everything has a price. The 2014 New York City Marathon stood between two very important traditions in our family, but once you get a spot in that race, you can't just give it up as if you can run that race any year you want. Those of us longing to win a spot from the lottery will do just about anything to get to that start line if we are able to get that bib.

The race was held on November 2, 2014. November 1st is Ethan's birthday; he would turn eight years old in New York. Halloween, of course, is October 31st; the kids would have to celebrate Halloween somewhere other than their own neighborhood, the place they have been every year for this candy collecting expedition. Ouch, are those pangs of guilt? Am I a bad mother for stepping over my traditions to run in one of the most iconic, and yet, *traditional* races of all time? I've seen it on television. Whole issues of *Runner's World* are devoted to this race, and even Seinfeld had us cheering for Jean Paul, who desperately didn't want to miss his start time again because, "Twas the volume" of his alarm clock, only to be handed a cup of hot tea from Kramer to miss the finish. I had visions of the bridge spans, the autumnal colored trees lining central park—so feeling like a bad mother or not, I *had* to do it.

Audrey had just turned ten and discovered how much she loved her friends, and she wanted to be at school all the time to be with them. If they let her sleep there, she would have. This was a new thing for David and me to see in her. Normally, if we had a family trip, that meant missing school, we got extra hugs. Not this time. She had major episodes of misery in New York, and never lost an opportunity to tell us what she was missing at school, and what all her friends were doing for Halloween. As pictures from events without her present rolled in, I heard it again, how I practically ruined fourth grade because of this race.

We did the best we could. The kids packed costumes, and we went to The Natural History Museum for their Halloween event. It turned out to be more fun than any of us had expected, and even Audrey found ways to be happy about it, even though her attitude started out quite grim.

Ethan was a good sport about his birthday. We found ways to make it special. I brought birthday decorations to set up in the room while he was sleeping the night before, so he had something to wake up to. David found a couple of restaurants that specialized in only macaroni and cheese, his all-time favorite meal, and we all really enjoyed that. The mac was followed by a trip to Times Square to see The Lion King and shop at Toys R Us—a pretty good birthday by any standards. That night, we found an Italian restaurant packed with carb-loading marathoners, and I slipped the number eight candle to our waiter for Ethan's birthday dessert. The whole restaurant sang along, including some marathoners straight from Italy, and he clearly looked happy, and felt special.

I hope someday, when they are older, they will look back and say, "Ohhh, I get it now. It *was* a big deal for Mom to run that race." And even though it was most certainly the experience of a lifetime, one that lived up to my dreams, I agree with the kids that there really is no place like home.

What made going home even more special to them, was that we got our first dog. A sweet little Bichon we named Benny. His name was decided while Audrey and I were reading The Boxcar Children one night. We kept thinking of good dog names for weeks, and as we read that book, when the name Benny appeared, we both looked at each other and yelled, "Benny!" We just knew.

Benny quickly became beloved by everyone. He is a sweet ball of white fluff. Well, truth be told, it took me a little while to adore him because, believe it or not, the kids promised with all their might, favorite stuffed animals as collateral, that they would help with the new puppy. Maybe you have heard this one before. But David had work, the kids were in school, and that left you-know-who to potty train this sweet puppy. As wonderful as dogs are, they require a lot of commitment, so it was an adjustment to have to leave events early, and basically plan everything around *when we would let the dog out*. Put your bib number back on, mom, you are back to the start line.

Benny, and all dogs, add an intangible type of life to a home. The kids loved playing with him, seeing him at the end of the day, and snuggling in bed with him while we read bedtime stories. Did I mention I was never going to let a dog on our furniture? Yes, ha-ha, very funny, I know.

Assuming we all agree on the value of consistency, we are also taught as runners that cross-training is essential for us to keep the links in the chain healthy. Particularly as we get older, it's very important to add some basic strength training into our fitness. I can really say this has been true for me. That miserable stress fracture and plantar fasciitis made that clear to me, and I can see increased strength and speed as a result of the cross-training.

The summer after my stress fracture was also the summer of my best abs, no kidding. I was surprised at what a big difference it made in my bat wings, and the cookie jar I call an abdomen.

Unfortunately, the very second that I slack off on abdominal work, my former six-pack quickly turns back into a keg, so I do try to keep a steady two-pack. On the days I lift weights or do body-weight strength moves, I continue to do them barefoot, and I have only slight flare-ups from the PF. Plus, it simply feels good mentally to do another activity once in a while. It forces different muscles to get active and let the over-used ones get a break.

.

Sometimes, we cross-train out of sheer desperation to move. If there is no one around to keep an eye on the kids, I can choose the elliptical, weights, or a video. So, if David wants to get in a run or some tennis with a neighbor on a Sunday before church, I don't belly-ache, because he also needs to take care of himself, since golfing doesn't really count as a cardio or strength program—it's okay, he knows.

I made a brief attempt to join the world of Cross-Fit. I won a package at a school fund-raising auction, and it was great timing since it was shortly after the 2013 Disney Marathon. time to back off on mileage and rebuild some of the beat-up spots. The trainer was a very nice, smart, beefcake of a girl, and seemed to have a balanced approach to this kind of fitness. She asked me if I did squats, and I said, "of course," overestimating my abilities. She asked me to demonstrate, so I did, and felt very confident in my strong runner's thighs. Then she said, "Oh. So you just bend your knees a little?"

"Well, yeah." But in an effort to play along, I went lower and lower so my bottom would graze the top of a stability ball, but I didn't like it. I realized within two visits that doing an impressively low squat was not worth blowing out a knee, and leaving me unable to run at all. *I keep up with Denise Austin and the gals from The Firm videos just fine, and they don't humiliate my apprehensive squats.*

I actually like workout videos, for many reasons: 1) No one can see how clumsy and uncoordinated I look following these moves in the privacy of my living room. 2) During the breaks between segments, I can run over and take laundry from the washer, and put it in the dryer. Moms love to multi-task. 3) It gives me a chance to think about what I might write in a thank-you note to Denise Austin for assisting in my increased duration when holding a plank.

But sometimes I overestimate my strength, and mess things up without anyone's help. After a few months of consistent weight training, I felt stronger, and even saw itty-bitty biceps start to bud. My abs said, "Hey, remember us? If you step back from the cookies, we'll come for a visit just in time for swimsuit season."

"Okay! Let's do this!" But, I did too much. I flung out weights in front of me at shoulder height, and felt the aftermath for over a week. It was too much weight, so the result was my back feeling like it was being ripped up both sides of my spine. It hurt to sit in the car, sit at dinner, and stand to do dishes. "Fine dishwasher, if you do your part, I'll do mine." But running is a miracle, because it was the one activity that didn't make me cry out in pain. We are so tough, but still so fragile.

After the 2014 Gasparilla Half Marathon here in Tampa, I was ready for a break from running. I got to that burned out point and knew it was time to back off for a few weeks, and pick up some weights for a while. In October 2013, during the Chicago marathon, I had some decent core strength to draw from toward the end of the race, but for this half, my core was nothing more than a family-sized bag of peanut butter M&M's. You can't chase down a PR from two years ago with chocolate sloshing around in your tummy. The very next day, I started with one of my easier weight training videos, and got to work.

I like to hop on the elliptical, because I can watch television and it has this cool "mix three" option that makes you go in reverse and then use only your arms, so it's a tiny bit entertaining.

A treadmill however, I have little comfort with. I use them at hotel gyms but that's about it. For one thing, I'm a bit clumsy, so I always feel a bit awkward getting started, and then trying to change the speed or the incline. Plus, if I make sudden movements on an already moving surface, I tend to feel dizzy, and even more likely to fall. I feel silly, or like I'm doing something wrong when I get the speed going a bit faster and it's shaking like an unbalanced washing machine. The treadmill also reminds me of my average day: Coffee, pack lunches, make breakfast, wake kids, help at school, run, errands, shower, laundry, get kids, homework, snack, break up the 5:00 p.m. fights, bath, dinner, reading, and bed. It's the same route over and over again, and I want to be free! Let me go down this street, I've never seen those houses before!

A lot of runners love the mill, depend on it, and it's their only method of getting a run in. I give these runners a lot of credit for sticking with it. Though having run through Buffalo winters and Florida summers, I am sure there would be an advantage to having an option of getting a forty-five-minute run in on a mill with climate control, instead of running around in khakis and a kerchief.

In the marathon training programs, there are cut-back weeks, where you run slightly less mileage to give your body a little rest, before making another push forward in the long run distance. In the same way, I try to let the kids have some cut-back moments from their hectic lives once in a while. Maybe I'll surprise the kids with a mid-week, after school ice cream or movie. They are so happy when they get an unexpected break from their own routines. Like a quick three-miler, it improves everyone's outlook and always ends up being a happy memory. They still have to get their things done, but we slow the pace down just a little and take a few breaths.

During high school, my mom surprised me with a random day off from school once a year, to spend time together. One time it was a drive to Niagara Falls, other times we hung out at home, watching movies in our pj's all day. The point was not the activity itself, but the shift of direction from our normal day, and having time to hang out together. One October, the kids had a long weekend off school. David was out of town, and I wanted to do some unusual activities, so one of the activities was having a camp-out in the family room. We made s'mores, with the help of the broiler, watched a movie, and snuggled. At 1:00 o'clock in the morning, I realized Ethan's air mattress had a slow leak and he was on the floor, with only a layer of vinyl underneath him, so I carried him into his bed. He was a DNF, Did Not Finish, for the camp-out.

Our own cut-backs from the normal chores of mothering are important too. My personal favorite is date night. I love going out to dinner with David, and chatting about everything happening in our lives. Sometimes it's just a bunch of nonsense, like quoting *Caddy Shack* lines while we people watch. We love to go out with other couples and swap stories of our kids' antics, as well as their accomplishments. Of course, the antics are always funnier and better for bonding. I find it's not just *my* kid that sneaks the hammer to pummel rocks in the driveway.

At least put on some goggles, please. The point is, although runners do find comfort and necessity in routine, stepping out once in a while can rejuvenate us for another push.

Just getting out the door for date night is a completely different kind of work-out. Like a race, but with a strict, almost impossible time limit. Reservations are for a certain time, the sitter is arriving at a certain time, and I still have to prepare dinner for the kids, write their bedtime notes, pack my phone and lip-gloss, and attempt to look glamorous in something other than a T-shirt and khaki shorts. I cram my lumps and bumps into shape wear, choose a relatively cool outfit, and try to get out of the house on time. As I run circles around the house, I casually ask, "Hey, Honey? Are you enjoying Sports Center?" This is the guy who'll be backing out of the garage, wondering what took me so long, as I trip out the door, carrying my heels and glistening, on the verge of a dripping sweat, depending on what time of year it is. Moms want the details covered.

One way I am able to break out of the normal hustle and bustle is on Mother's Day. Our loved ones always want to know what it is that would make us happy and re-energized, and for me, that is the *I Love Mother's Day 5-K* at John Chestnut Park, in Palm Harbor, Florida. The park where it's held is packed with trees and trails, and it reminds me a little bit of running up north. I slip out before anyone is up, drive quietly with my coffee to the park, get checked in, and enjoy the lake views from the tree canopied park. An added bonus is that the park is equipped with clean bathrooms. And there is a trumpeter who plays "When the Saints Go Marching In" for us at the start line —I certainly won't argue with that.

After the race, I walk around a bit, and enjoy chatting with the other runners and being in the natural surroundings before heading home. On the way, I stop to pick up donuts and surprise them, as they prepare my *surprise* breakfast and giant

Happy Mother's Day sign. It's a perfect morning combination of consistent running and a cut-back from making breakfast. Of course, it won't be a surprise when I realize that I'll probably have to clean it up because everyone is headed outside to play.

After training for a race, especially the longer ones, we take a pause, and we enter the cut-back period of running fewer miles to give our bodies a break and replenish our glycogen stores. It is also known as "Taper Madness," because although it sounds like it should be a relief and a welcome break, it can be frustrating. This is especially true for first-time marathoners because you may feel like you're not doing enough—not an easy emotion for a mom to navigate. I was worried that I was going to lose all the strength and endurance I worked so hard to claim. I had to give up control for a few weeks, and trust Mr. Higdon and all his years of running wisdom that I would be ready for the race. I realized that the taper is ultimately an issue of trust and honesty with oneself. If you followed the plan and stayed healthy, you can expect to run a great race. But if you were constantly nursing injuries, or slacked off on workouts, then you can't expect to run a personal best. Your race-day goal has to be changed accordingly.

Physically, the taper is for our bodies to recover and rest adequately for a good race. Not that we just get to flop down on the couch and veg out, because the extra time on our hands is quickly filled. I use some of the marathon taper time to prepare my race-day gear. I make sure there are enough packets of fuel, decent socks to wear, and any race information organized in one place. If the weather looks like it might be a problem, I fish out old clothes I can throw away on the course, and pick up a few inexpensive rain ponchos from the drugstore.

I use some of the time to catch up on projects that may have been neglected around the house. That last month of training is the most intense, and things don't always get done like normal. I find it relaxing to give the house, and its contents, some order once again. I usually help at school a little more if they need volunteers, and even see friends for lunch. Moms all get so busy that sometimes our friendships taper during seasons of the year. No one has a lot of time to do anything outside their world of responsibilities, but when some time does open up, it sure is revitalizing to hang with the girls and catch up with each other's stories.

I try to remember that as my miles decrease, so should my calories. It is very easy to get accustomed to luxurious portions of even our healthy foods, but going from forty miles a week, to twenty, means fewer chunks of feta on that salad, and no more using Doritos as croutons. The taper period for the Disney Marathon is always during the Christmas and New Year's holidays, which means all the best goodies of the year are hanging out, and available at every gathering. "Get away from me, cheese platter! I don't think we've met, spinach and artichoke dip, I am in the taper, so we'll have to get acquainted some other time."

Motherhood is one giant taper, even among wildlife. Florida is home to an abundance of interesting tropical birds, and one of our favorites is the Sand Hill Crane. These gray birds get to be about four feet tall, and have bodies so large that it's hard to imagine them being able to fly. They have some red feathers on their heads and make a unique sound like a high-pitched rolling of the Spanish letter 'r.' What we love the most is how they travel as a family. In our neighborhood, they walk silently in slow motion through our driveways, yards, roads, wherever they want. They sit in groups under our trees and occasionally come up to our front door. When I am out running, or we are on a family walk or bike ride, they are completely calm. While most birds and small animals scurry out of sight, these cranes casually walk like they have all the time in the world and there is no way they'd be scared of one striding runner in a cap and mismatched outfit. Just like in the advertisements for Easter dresses, filled with baby chicks, the springtime here brings baby Sand Hill Cranes. The babies are shorter, thinner, yellow, and temptingly fuzzy. The families tend to travel the same routes, so we get to see the growth of the babies. As the yellow fades and they get a bit taller, Audrey calls that the teenager stage. This growth happens quicker than we expect and eventually, the teenager Sand Hill Cranes are grown-up, able to take care of themselves, and are off starting their own families.

After Audrey was born, she and I were together all the time, just like the Sand Hill Cranes. I took her everywhere I was allowed to bring a child, and had babysitters very sparingly. I was enamored with this child and truly enjoyed being with her. The same was true for Ethan. While at the playgrounds, I proudly had him in the front-carrying-pack like a badge of honor. I could hold his little feet and simultaneously encourage Audrey on the slides.

With the pre-programmed words of, "I can do it myself!" continuously on repeat, they began to attempt everything, from putting on a DVD and knowing which buttons to press, to pouring a glass of milk from a full gallon jug. Even though we could see the spill was inevitable, we hovered but zipped our lips so they could learn from the different experiences. It didn't take long for them to know when to ask for help, and when they could handle something on their own. As the months of their early years rolled on, they were getting their own snacks, tying their own shoes, and even reading. There was nothing for me to do but put my feet up and read magazines with a can of nuts and a cool glass of lemonade.

Well, not exactly. The simpler tasks of motherhood, once you finally get comfortable with them, get replaced with responsibilities of greater difficulty. We teach them how to share, use good manners, and how to handle a kid who is not so nice on a playground. Then it's deciding what music and movies are okay for them, and sending them off for their very first sleepover. Tapering from one activity usually means spending more time in new ones.

When I enrolled Audrey in pre-school, I most certainly cried and felt her absence around the house, but I knew I would be an involved mom throughout the kids' school years. I had the security blanket of helping several times a week with story time and class parties, and being able to see them in their element.

There will always be copies to make and funds to raise, but opportunities to hover over them at school are most certainly dwindling. I have to go through this part of the training, and trust that I completed each week of the plan the best I could, that I did everything I could to have a great race.

At the ice-skating rink, Audrey saw a younger male friend she made during her skating and hockey periods, so she went to say hello. An older boy came by, and the three of them were talking like they had known each other for years. This took me by surprise for some reason. I knew she had friends, was very confident, and social. But she was also very much a homebody, and very content to spend a lot of time with the family. This was a first glimpse of the fact that the time is coming that my presence won't be needed anymore and unwelcome even. I held back, skated with Ethan, and let her have her time with her friends but it was tough to start giving some space. I suppose that is part of the goal—that they will be fine on their own, but it feels as fast as the short few weeks of growth of a Sand Hill Crane.

The tangible reminder of their growth is that their clothing becomes too small for their newer bodies, right on schedule, time after time, and usually when their shorts can't hold even one more mud stain. Audrey has had her last of the kids' store pajamas, and has started sleeping in T-shirts and athletic shorts.

One night during this transition, all of her sleepwear was still in the dryer, so I offered her a pair of my pajama shorts. Coincidentally, they were the *Today Show* pajama shorts I bought on our trip to New York when she was only three. Now stood before me this very tall, strong girl in my shorts. They were really way too big, but with the drawstring, they worked. It made me take a pause, to notice what's going on around here. It's not good-bye to childhood, but hello to this fascinating new person they become each day.

Chapter 9
Negative Splits

Runners are absolutely obsessed with time. We want to save time by running the tangents, skipping the aid stations and wearing as little as possible on race day. We place an extreme amount of hope on a few tiny seconds. Before the 2013 Chicago Marathon, friends asked if I had any goals in mind for the race. Having run a 4:01 at the 2013 Disney Marathon, my goal was very simple. "As long as my net time reads 3:59:59, I'll be happy. The few seconds that would grant me the title of, "Sub Four-Hour Marathoner" would make me very happy indeed. But it seems so silly to most normal people, that a minute and a half could somehow exalt you to a higher category in your own mind. But it does. We are measured by time.

Our goals and personal competitiveness make us ask ourselves, "What is my average minute-per-mile pace?" "How fast do I have to do these speed-repeats?" "How can I beat my past time for this course?" "How can I get my time down to qualify for Boston?" And the most important of all, "When will I *have* time to run this week?"

In addition to consuming our normal range of food and wearing our tried-and-true gear the day of a race, the running experts tell us that to run our personal best, we are encouraged to finish the second half of the race slightly faster than the first, known as running negative splits. We should start out a bit slower than we think we should, to conserve energy for the later miles of the race, and to feel great mentally with a strong, powerful finish, rather than the kind of final miles where you are deciding which of your running shoes you'll burn first. It sounds like a good idea but feels counterintuitive. "Shouldn't I run the whole thing at my fastest speed possible?" It makes us think that easing up on pace will keep us from hitting a time goal. But it does work, and I have actually been able to achieve this at some races. Sometimes, through dumb luck, like the races that are so crowded in the start and you can do little more than walk for a while anyway, which forces me to hold back a little.

But sometimes I try to fight through the crowds too fast, and spend far too much valuable glycogen trying to get around runners and move laterally to find an open space for some elbowroom. The Gasparilla Half Marathon in Tampa is where I do this, hopping up and down on street curbs like an idiot, as though I might be a contender for a prize. The only prize that it will actually get me is a good old-fashioned fall on the face, and a possible DNF. This, of course, is a horrible strategy, and I don't recommend it because it's a total waste of energy. Fighting for time is tricky because time doesn't have to stop for Gatorade, or a picture with the kids, or a visit to the porta-potty. Time doesn't have variables like wind, uncomfortable shorts, chafing, or a bad night's sleep. It keeps going at an even pace, all the time.

When you cross the finish line, that's it. The race is done. It's a very temporary piece of time that can elate us or haunt us as we review our effort. All we can do is look back at a race or a training plan, and evaluate what went wrong, and how we could do better next time.

A goal that I didn't have for the 2013 Chicago Marathon was to qualify for Boston. I just didn't see how it could happen, unless I had put in some serious speed work, and everything for race day was 100% perfect. But, as I was running and looking at the pace display on my GPS watch, around mile thirteen I thought, "Holy cow, maybe I can do this. Don't get too excited, there's a long way to go." But I didn't listen, and I got *very* excited. I even felt more energy at the mere thought of reaching that kind of time. With Justin Timberlake's "Rock Your Body" song going through my head, I just kept plugging along, thinking, "Maybe..."

But around mile nineteen, I started making some deals with myself. "Okay, you can back off for a few miles, recover a bit, and then get back to a good pace."

"Okay," I answered. "Sounds fair."

"Hey! And get those knees up, engage your core, and pay attention." Well, once you start making deals with yourself, that's pretty much it. time doesn't make deals. I knew I wouldn't make the qualifying time but I wasn't at all sad. I still cranked out a 3:48, a little more than three minutes from the Boston Qualifying (BQ) time for my age group that year and a huge PR (personal record).

Reviewing the race, there was very little I could have done to recoup over three minutes. I didn't have to stop for a restroom break, I carried my own water bottle and only stopped twice to fill up, the weather was basically perfect, and I was happy with no injuries. So, with all the factors being as good as they can ever get, where do you get three and a half more minutes? If I ever find out, I'll let you know.

Otherwise, that race in particular was a bit of a blur. It all went by so fast, and I can only remember bits and pieces of the course. My focus was so singularly on the GPS pace display on my wrist that I didn't look around and absorb the whole experience of the race as I wish I had.

Some days are like that with the kids. I get on the daily treadmill, complete all the tasks, and suddenly it's, "When did you get so tall??" I often wonder—can I have both? Can I get everything done and really take a moment to enjoy it too?

I was lucky, and the kind of excited that made me barely able to talk about it without climbing out of my skin, to get a spot to run the New York Marathon in November 2014. After three years in the lottery, and using my one-time deferral allowance, I was now about to run *the dream.* So, I had to decide: Do I speed through this thing and try for a BQ, or PR? Or, do I deliberately slow way down and run it like a tourist, enjoying all the trappings, as it will likely be the only time I get to run in it?

I wish I had paid more attention to my surroundings in Chicago, but yet, I have this adorable 3:48 to cuddle with. Is it worth it to give up a competitive time for a good time? That is one of those questions for the ages.

There is a saying about motherhood, that the days are long but the years are short, and it really is true. When the kids were little, it took effort and deliberate planning to fill the day with meals, naps, and activities, but the weeks seemed to just melt away, like picking up sand at the beach and watching it slip through your fingers. I was speeding through those days, and even more so now with the addition of their homework, friends, and activities. Yet, as they grow, I hear myself saying things to make the theory of negative splits work in real time. "Hurry up and finish your homework so we have more time later!" Really? That doesn't even sound possible. We can't make, as in create, more time. But we push our little ones out the door to get to school on time and continue to nag them to "move along," even though Ethan just found a really cool leaf and has to stop to pick it up. Mr. Williams would appreciate that he is looking at the foliage.

I have been watching Audrey grow, as reflected on her choice of wall "decorations." We moved into our home when she was just under two, and her walls were painted pink. I chose a quilt and bedding that had light green, some yellow, bits of blue, but all very subtle and classic so as not to have to get a new comforter every time she had a new favorite TV show character. When she was about five, she realized she could hang things of her own choosing in her room. We are very generous with the use of tape around here, and I even use masking tape for many Christmas decorations. She taped up her drawings and colored pictures that were all *Toy Story* movie characters. Even on her bed frame, she wrote the name *Buzz*, but here z's were still backwards so it looks like *Buss*. So cute. By the time she was six, I found that her *Toy Story* exhibit was being reduced, and collections of *Star Wars* images were granted generous wall space.

By the age of seven, all previous artwork was removed, and in its place was everything hockey. She asked to have her room painted light blue, and to have Tampa Bay Lightning Fatheads everywhere. Okay, it's your room, and it's a reasonable request. Instead of being displayed with pink grosgrain ribbon, the letters of her name on the wall now hang from a horizontally placed hockey stick. She has homemade posters like the ones the fans bring to games, reading, "Go Bolts!" She has asked for new bedding, which I have yet to allow because her tastes do change rather quickly, and when she was nine and a half, I was given a tour of her newest art, pictures of the members of the band One Direction. *Gulp*. My throat is tightening, it's all happening too fast, please someone stop the clock.

Ethan and I were on a drive to a field trip recently, traveling on roads that we take only once or twice a year. As we passed the location of a museum we had visited with some friends, I pointed in that direction and said, "Ethan, do you remember we went to the museum with Ella and saw the planetarium inside, and the log boats, and manatees?"

"Did it have the stingrays?"

Sheila Scott

"No buddy, but it did have the big dinosaur skeleton in front, and we ate lunch in the car because we couldn't find a picnic spot."

He furrowed his eyebrows, trying to bring up the memory from his little file cabinets. "A little."

"Wow, was that last summer or the one before?" I wondered. "Oh my goodness, I think it was *three* summers ago! Holy cow, where does the time go?"

"I don't know, Mommy. Are we almost to the field trip yet?"

"Almost, Monkey, almost. We'll be there before you know it."

Ethan lost three top teeth within a week and a half. The little-boy smile that pierced my heart for seven years was forever gone, and a new smile emerged, crooked for a long while, but that would be cute and innocent in its own way too. Take the pictures while you can, it will change as soon as you turn your back.

Sometimes at lunch somewhere or in church, I will see a young woman there, with the little basket car seat containing a small infant. I like to watch the little legs move involuntarily back and forth, kicking off a sock, always only one for some reason, and the blanket coverings bubbling around. It's so adorable. And I love when the mom picks the baby up and the baby's head wobbles around while trying to locate a thumb or chew toy. I always think I should helpfully offer to hold her baby while she is eating because I remember what a chore that was, but I realize I would probably look a little suspicious, so I keep my mouth shut, and smile politely. I think about how she has no idea what short moments these are, as she casually places the baby back in the seat, and gently rocks it back and forth while chatting with her friend. Running in a long race, you think you have plenty of time to look around and soak in the experience. But suddenly, those three, thirteen, or twenty-six miles are done. The volunteers are packing up, the cups are swept up, and it went much faster than you thought. Then you think, "Mile two was so crowded, but it looked pretty. Can I run mile two again?"

Despite my warm and happy memories of my kids' early years, I adjusted rather quickly to them starting school. I shed my fair share of tears, and I missed having lunch with them, and having the freedom of making our own schedule. But I soon realized that I could get a few things done, and even occasionally go out to lunch, grateful that, for a change, I wasn't the woman on her hands and knees picking up broken crayons and french fries.

I had always taken them everywhere with me. Chiropractor visits, hair appointments, and all of the errands moms have. Especially Audrey, since she was the only one for a while. I even took her to my C-section pre-operation appointment before Ethan was born. Not by choice, but by last resort. For weeks, David had it on his schedule to be home with Audrey so I could go to this appointment alone. Just hours prior to my appointment, I got the call that some big-wig was in town for a last-minute meeting—he *had* to meet with this guy. With such short notice, a sitter was not an option, so I had to pack half the house to keep her entertained, and plenty of snacks. We waited an unbelievable two hours before the nurse called me in for the appointment. We took little walks around the hospital lobby, colored, read books, and went to the potty about eighty-five times. Audrey was surprisingly good the whole time, and it was all going very smoothly. I even set aside a little stash of candy corns to hand her as soon as I really needed to pay attention. Unfortunately, just as the really important part of the consultation began, she had her meltdown. That was it—she was tired, fed up, and ready to leave. Even the candy corns did not buy me any more chip time. I remember the nurse mumbling something about "being gutted like a fish," and the rest was unheard. The truth is, even if you can take your kids to do all this stuff, it's just easier without them.

The first time I went to the mall on a weekday without my kids, I was a bit misty at the sight of all the moms meeting with their strollers in the play areas, but it dawned on me... "Wait! Let me get this straight...I can try on a pair of shorts without a child crawling underneath the other fitting rooms?! Is it true that no one will tell me they have to use the potty while I'm trying on jeans? This is fantastic!"

It's not just shopping for clothes or groceries that fill our weeks. Every stay-at-home mom has been asked at least once this question: "What do you do all day?"

Seriously? "You can't believe what I accomplish by 10:00 a.m. most days," is the start of my answer, and as I go through the list of an average day, they look exhausted just thinking about it. What no one seems to realize about the school day, is how it too goes by *so fast.* By the time you subtract commuting time, you are left with about six and a half hours, which sounds like a lot, but it really isn't. Subtract time for a workout and a shower, and you're down to five hours. Add in cleaning, errands, chaperoning for a field trip, dealing with the "problem of the week," be it septic tank gurgles or the bug guy helping tame the fire ants, and yard work, the day is gone.

I am highly motivated by the threat of having to bring the kids with me to do errands. If I could avoid having to lead my flock of two into Walgreens, where they will inevitably beg for gum, candy, or a stretchy plastic toy that will break before we get home, I'll do almost anything to achieve that goal. They are good kids, they really are, but they are *kids.* They seem to always have to go to the bathroom, especially as I'm taking the groceries from the cart to the conveyor belt. When I have to get information from the car mechanic, it's best if I listen, but also tough to do when they are constantly interrupting, or worse, starting to fight.

Because of my ability to pack minutes with as much stuff as possible, I mostly feel bad for the cashiers, or other shoppers near me during the week. After the kids are safely in their class-rooms with all their necessities, I take off on a run for four to twenty miles, depending on the time of year. If I go all the way home to shower at this point, I lose a ton of time, and likely get distracted by projects needing attention at the house. In real life, the clock time and the chip time are one in the same. At least in a race, if you can limit any stopping, your chip time will be better than your clock time. I want to save every precious minute, so I keep packages of unscented baby wipes in the car with some dry clothes, and then start my to-do list. Once the list is complete, I hurry to make it home in time for a quick shower and to turn back around to get the kids. And as the time wears on, so does the awful post-run aroma. But if you stand too close to me at the post office after a run, don't say I didn't warn you.

And, like the final sprint to the finish line, some of our biggest life moments happen in split seconds. Audrey was just a couple of months old, laying on her back on the mat with the hanging toys for her to swat at. I was nearby, dusting, folding laundry, and tidying up. I kept looking over at her and chatted the usual "goos" and "who's my girl?" in my cheerful mommy voice. I turned my back for one second to pick up a fallen sock, and she was now on her tummy. Just like that, I missed it. I was with her every second of every day, and still missed the effort and movement it took for her to flip herself over for the very first time.

She did that to me again a few months later when I placed her in her crib to sit while I put away new diapers and wipes. By the time I turned around to pick her up to change her, she was standing there, holding onto the crib railing, toothy and proud. *Unbelievable.*

She did redeem herself one summer when Ethan was about eight months old. Our pool has a large, wide step at the entry, which is a great spot for kids to sit and play, or grown-ups to cool off without getting soaked. I sat Ethan there with some toys, as he was strong and able to sit steadily on his own, while I swept some of the patio about four steps from him. Audrey rushed to his side, pushed him up, and called out to me, "Mommy, Ethan was falling but I saved him!" I was standing *right there* and almost missed the whole thing. Scary split-seconds.

My own split-second mishap took place the day I was set to complete my twenty-mile training run for the 2011 Space Coast Marathon. After already dropping Audrey off at her school for first grade, Ethan was with me in the car, and we were on the way to his half-day preschool. I planned to walk him in, start the run, and let him stay for the Lunch Bunch group so I could finish the last big run. A few yards from my left turn into the parking lot, on a tree-lined road with no shoulder, I looked down at the passenger seat for a paper I needed to give his teachers. By the time I looked up, after that apparently lengthy second, I realized I was not going to have time to stop before crashing into either the stopped car waiting to turn left in front of me, or the trees on the right. Both terrible choices, I slammed on the brakes and aimed for the trees. *Again* with these trees. My logic was that I'd rather apologize to a tree than a busy mom taking her kids to preschool.

The airbags did their job. Ethan and I got some scrapes from the seatbelts but we were otherwise completely safe. I brought him into school, where they comforted him with ice packs and popsicles so I could go outside and tell the police officers that I flaked out. Split seconds.

I called David, who, much to my relief, happened to be in town, and I told him what happened. "Hi, it's me. Are you busy?" I casually asked.

"A little, but what's up?"

"Well, we're okay, but I crashed my car into a tree."

"Oh no, where are you? Are the kids with you?! Are any of you hurt?!"

"We are totally fine. Audrey is already at school. It happened right before I was supposed to turn into Ethan's school. He's fine, I brought him inside already. I looked down for a paper I needed to bring in this morning and didn't see the car breaking in front of me. I didn't have enough time to fully stop, so instead of hitting that mom's car, I chose the tree."

"Oh, thank God you are alright. Can you back it out?" he asked, not getting a clear visual of what I had just done.

"Ummm, definitely not, it looks like the engine is on the ground, and the airbags popped."

"Oh. Okay, I'll leave the office in five minutes."

"Thank you. Oh, here come the police officers, I gotta go."

When he got there, he handled all the business of things and showed the insurance cards, and he waited for the tow-truck to haul away my freedom on four wheels. The first thing that I thought about once Ethan was safe and the car was being pulled from its nest was, "When on earth will I have time to do this twenty-miler this weekend?" Not only that, but when you are preparing all your fuel, water bottles, and running gear, you are also preparing mentally for the hours stretched out ahead of you. Having to reschedule made me very anxious. So, while I contemplated the realization that I will have to get myself psyched up all over again to cover these miles, David came over and asked, "So, are you okay?"

"Oh, yeah, I'm fine. I feel bad for Ethan, though. I hope he's not scared."

"I'm sure he's okay. Let's go get him and just get you two home."

"Okay, that sounds good since I don't have time to get twenty miles in at this point."

"Well, if you're okay, do you mind dropping me at the golf

course? I'm supposed to play with some clients today, and you can keep my car for the day," he carefully asked.

"No problem, as long as you can be home in the morning so I can get these twenty in from today. I'll be out the door by 6:30 a.m."

"Deal. Take your time, and start a little later so you can rest more," he added for a bonus. Sometimes we do find ways to make more time.

Of course, all these things get recorded in our training logs so that when race day comes, I can review my workouts and convince myself that I'm prepared to run my goal time. The first training log was the most ornate and detailed, where I recorded things like the weather, or the *Very Important Reason* I had to miss a run. The second one was almost as nice, but a little lighter on details, and the three after that were simply amounts of miles and dates. These are very similar to the baby books and scrapbooks. The first few for each child certainly were more ornate in their creation, and the later years are pictures and a few quick notes.

Like reviewing the training logs or races, each with their successes and trouble spots, I look through these books containing the big and small moments of the kids, and see what I've done. I try to look at the tough miles and weak performances, and train better for the next race. Running mixes up my sense of time, in that it makes me feel much younger than I am, so I think I have all this time to fix my mistakes and do better in the next race. But there are only so many more races, and school plays, the huge clock timer above the start line just keeps going, so whatever needs tweaking, it's time to get it done now. If you need to work on your downhill technique or make time for one more bedtime story, this is it. But even when my miles aren't so perfect, I keep moving forward.

Chapter 10
Mom-entum with Our Missions

I try to avoid sitting down during the day, especially on really busy days. Like, when I have to stop running to wait to cross a busy road, it's sometimes tough to get back in that flow, the momentum of my movement. My thighs might speak up and say, "Hey, aren't we done here? What's going on?" It's easier to just keep going until I know I can be done for the day. So, if I see a fifteen-minute chunk of time open up, I pretend we don't own a couch, because if I fall asleep and miss picking up the kids on time from school, boy will they be upset.

Much of our daily mundane activities, such as picking up kids, go largely unnoticed and very often taken for granted. And that's okay because we know that if we suddenly decided to stop doing even one of our chores, the house would be total mayhem. Napping through pick-up would create a domino effect of untold ferocity. I am certain that when David is kind enough to empty the dishwasher, I can count on twenty percent of those items getting left on the counter, neatly placed, but homeless and lonely, because after being in our home for eight years, he still doesn't know where some of our cooking implements live. Moms are the flexible joints that keep the mundane links in our family chain moving steadily and smoothly.

In addition to keeping our family life at an even pace, we moms love to chip in to help in many other ways, oftentimes through the sport we love. According to RunningUSA.org, forty-three percent of all marathon finishers in 2013 were females, and eighty-four percent of those women were between the ages of twenty-five and fifty-four, typical for the mom years. Just as cool as those numbers, Running USA reports that 2013 was the first time ever that women finishers in the half-marathon hit a whopping sixty percent. We are out there, ladies.

Of the forty-five thousand runners at the 2013 Chicago Marathon, ten thousand of those were running with a charity team, and the 2014 New York City Marathon has over two hundred different charities represented, supporting everything from animal services, to local food banks, to organizations aimed at the cure of present-day diseases. For some runners, their alliance with an organization isn't about money at all, but to raise awareness about a hidden societal problem and get people talking. For some, a race is a run in private honor of a loved one, to leave a heap of heavy sorrows on the hot pavement. At the root of it all is a deep passion for a mission, and every mile counts. The common goal is to make something better, so we find another store of energy to improve the things that touch our hearts.

Our mom missions aren't limited to raising money for a bib number. I have spent countless hours at my kids' school organizing parties, fundraisers, creating artwork for auctions, and making copies for the teachers whose time is stretched to transparency. I actually like the backstage jobs at school because those are the ones that often directly benefit the teachers or students. The only volunteer jobs that I can't stand are the ones where I feel like there is nothing for me to do. It is frustrating when there are too many of us, to do too few jobs. If I am going to give you my time, please put me to work. Standing around thinking of what else I could be doing is like standing on a non-moving treadmill.

Our church offers a weeklong evening sports camp for kids each summer. They start with a light dinner, and enjoy the benefit of late-day outside sports, which is a kindness in Florida, as the summer days are intensely hot. I serve on the food service team, which is one of the busiest groups to be in. The kids stare at us while they wait in line, and pray we don't run out of Chick-fil-A sandwiches. After the evidence of dinner for hundreds is quickly cleaned up, and while the kids are out on the fields, we lug coolers of popsicles to each group to provide much-needed hydration for the little athletes. All those years of waitressing for Ramen Noodle money in college gave me skills to use to help others. I never saw that coming.

When our church needs six-dozen cookies for an event, I fire up the mixer, since I can finally bake proudly. And when they need thousands of candleholders cleaned out for Christmas Eve service, I scrape wax while watching some evening television. Little stuff, but it helps ease someone else's load.

I began a new leadership role in my Bible study, where I facilitate discussion groups each week. I was reluctant when asked if I wanted to take on this role because my first thought was, "Where am I going to find the time to do this?" But it somehow appears and blends in with my schedule. And while it's technically a service to others, I know that it is an opportunity for me to grow in a new way, as volunteering usually is.

We have to pick and choose how often we say yes, because it doesn't take long until a committee pegs us as a cheerful, willing volunteer. Chair people have file folders with target symbols containing our faces. "Oh, she'll help, she does a great job with the booster club!" Which is why, if it always seems like the same group of volunteers over and over—it is.

Sheila Scott

Although not a huge act of service to the world, one of my most memorable was while I served as room mother for Audrey's second grade year. Memorable because of the fear and panic I felt, and the anxiety of putting my weak artistic skills on public display. Our jobs for the school year included things such as stuffing weekly informational parent folders, gathering donations and volunteers for class parties, and producing a class artwork piece for our annual fundraising auction. The one requisite of the piece was that it had to equally represent each student in that particular class. Some moms were ambitious enough to transform unfinished picnic tables, rocking chairs, and toy chests into sentimental, functional art, using finger-prints, handprints, or smaller individual pieces of art, and of course lots and lots of paint. Not I, said the fly. My main requi-site was that it had to be something that I could carry, and would be easy to transport back and forth to school as needed for the decorating process. I chose to create a large flowerpot. It seemed like a great idea as I admired so many pretty landscapes while running in different neighborhoods. And since Floridians are outside much of the year, I imagined it gracing someone's patio or front step, evoking warm memories of childhood. Ahh, if only it had been as easy as the plan in my mind.

Upon researching how to accomplish this great idea, it was once again confirmed that I am not a craft expert, other than the small ones I do with the kids to keep them busy. The terra-cotta pot had to be washed, wiped, and primed before the first drip of paint went on. It took forever to dry between coats, and once I could finally start applying real paint, I learned after a few coats by hand with a brush, that I was getting nowhere other than to a streaky, cheap looking mess. They make this stuff look so easy on HGTV, wearing their cute outfits and not a hint of panic in their faces. Grasping at straws, in fear of having to come up with another idea entirely and complete it in a short period of time, I decided to try a can of spray paint. What a relief. Nice even coats, and a smooth base surface were at last achieved.

To make it unique to the class, I cut out tree shapes from thick green paper, and had each child write, in pencil, what makes them grow. As in, "Audrey grows with hugs from dad, and hockey games." Cute. Once their writing was done in pencil to allow for corrections, they were asked to draw over their words with a black permanent marker, at which point I would attach the trees to the outside of the pot, add the final decorative details, and seal the whole thing up for outdoor use. Sadly, some students used washable marker instead of permanent, which I discovered as I began spreading the first coat of many of the sealing product over their writing. *Ughh!* Not only was this product making a cloudy film over everything, dab, dab, dab, it was making the ink run from the washable markers. I begged out loud, "Nooo! Please ink, stay, please don't run!" From that point on, I had to individually dab, dab, dab the trees with the washable marker very carefully to get them to the point of being covered enough to get a good final few coats of proper sealing product. This whole project probably took about two months of me being hopped up on sealant fumes. It did end up raising a good amount of money at the auction, and I was grateful to have any bidders, otherwise that sure would have been embarrassing. I hoped the winner wouldn't try to get a refund. After having had it for a year, I asked the mom who won it, "So. How's the pot? Did it melt yet?" She laughed and said it was fine and has even been in full sunlight all this time. That was a relief. What I learned is this: The seemingly simple and effortless ideas you get while wearing running shoes don't always work out so easily in real life, and that if I am ever room mom again, I will delegate the craft job to someone more capable.

I was a beneficiary of another mom's selfless and unnoticed act of service, one that was a great example of kindness, and helped solidify my future as a lifelong runner. My parents were divorced, and my mom often worked two jobs to earn enough income. That meant she wasn't able to attend more than a handful of my races through all of high school. My dad worked several towns over and was also only able to attend a few. It didn't hurt my feelings, because I understood my situation; I didn't take it personally. It was also the nineteen eighties in a small town so we were used to independence. It only became a problem my senior year because my mom's second job began at a time that would require her to be at work, and not available to pick me up from practice every day. I was devastated at the thought of missing my senior year with the cross-country team. I considered walking home after practice, as I had done from all my part time jobs, but it was four miles from school, which would take at least an hour walking with a backpack full of homework, so not a great option. And suffice it to say, there was no financial way of having my own car. I could have biked home, but that would have required biking to school and ruining the huge feathered bangs we all worked so hard on in those days. No dice.

I decided to show up for practice and try to get a ride home from different parents of teammates each day. After a few weeks, my teammate Heidi's mom took notice of the pattern and asked me if I needed a ride home every day. I explained my circumstances, and just like that, she brought me home every day after practice for the rest of the season. While as an adult, I am well aware there are far worse obstacles people overcome each day in the name of living, let alone running, but to me, at that time, it was like a suitcase of anxiety had been taken from my weakening grip. I no longer had to come up with a plan to beg for a ride home the next day. I lived a few miles out of their way home, so it was definitely extra time for her, but she never complained or made me feel like an obligation.

Being a polite kid, I thanked her each day as I stepped out of her minivan, but I know that I will never be able to really thank her for giving me that last season with the team. Tears well up in my eyes to this day when I think about what she did for me, because it's one of those small seeds, a tiny act of service that has an effect that the planter doesn't always get to see decades later. We can never say, "Oh, that won't make a big difference to someone, so why bother?" Every small thing really does make a ripple—even a simple car ride. Imagine how many little things you have already done for someone that will still touch her heart many years from now. Probably a lot, and we moms have a lot of opportunities to help a harrier out.

A few years later, as a college senior, our sorority volunteered to help at water stations for the 1994 Buffalo Marathon in early May. We had to report to the coordinator extremely early, and we had most likely been out late the night before, or more likely early that morning, since the bars in Buffalo were open until 4:00 a.m. On Saturday nights, our philanthropic missions were directed to those establishments for their five-dollar plastic cups that we could fill with as much beer and drinks as possible. We also generously supported our favorite all-night breakfast places once the bars stopped filling up our cups. It's so important to be a patron of local businesses.

Because we were young and well-trained with late nights, we made it on time and were sent to our various stations along the route. I must have been assigned to a later mile aid-station because I remember just waiting and waiting, and making small talk with the other volunteers. Fortunately, the weather was great, even warm for early May in Buffalo, probably near seventy degrees, and even sunny. We received instructions on how to hand a runner his or her water cup, be careful with the rake when clearing cups between packs, and to remember to cheer enthusiastically for all the runners that came through.

Finally, the first runners were approaching, and we were to begin serving our purpose, ready with plenty of prepared cups.

These guys were flying. I was in complete awe that they could run that fast for that many miles, it didn't seem possible. We had guys that fast in high school but our races were only 3.1 miles— this was a whole different ball game. That first pack of runners was sparse, and many of them didn't stop for water, so we felt silly with all those cups sitting there. But it wasn't long before the rest of the field was on their way and we were jamming.

This was probably the first time the seed of running a marathon got deeply planted. Though at the time, my soil was rocky, so the seed just lay there, crowded by all the pizza and beer. But it was an inspiration, and even though I was still immature, I knew I was watching something special, and it stayed with me.

We were screaming, cheering, and handing out water cups like old pros. Our hands were wet and wrinkled, and as much as we were cheering on the runners and hoping to provide them a little encouragement, with each stride, they gave off an energy that surrounded us and made us want to work even harder. Though I didn't run a step that day, I had the runner's high through osmosis.

As races get bigger, even more volunteers are needed, and they are the real super-heroes of the day. The race organizers and volunteers are out setting up mile markers, water stations, and registration tables long before the runners arrive. Everything is ready for the participants, who rarely see a glimpse of how much work the volunteers have put in before they hand out the first cup of water. Plus, they stay long after runners drag themselves through the finishing area, to help clean up all the supplies.

The year I ran the New York City Marathon, runners were given an option of utilizing baggage check to store dry clothes after the race, or receive a fleece lined marathon poncho. Never passing up an opportunity for more swag, I chose the poncho option, and send a heart-felt thank you to the woman who helped me with it after the race. She called herself "The Poncho Mama." We were tired, frozen, spaced-out, and she wrapped me in warmth with her joy and kindness. Plus, it was a *really* cool poncho.

A few years ago, I helped hand out medals and collect place cards at our school fun run. These little, sweaty kids came through the chute, huffing and puffing with their red faces, and they took a quick second to remember their own name, since they hadn't quite figured out correct pacing, beyond *push as hard as you can for as long as you can.* Soon, the glow of pride beamed through their eyes as they realized what they just accomplished. The PE coaches who set this up even gave three-deep gender and age-group awards to each, the two-mile, the mile, and the half-mile, and the top finishers got their moment in the spotlight among their peers. Untold seeds of inspiration were planted in their hearts.

I also like to plant seeds of running to anyone who will listen, and make it my mission to convince others of the magnificence and simplicity of our sport. At school, most of the moms know I run since I am always fleeing the scene on foot once the kids are where they need to be. Occasionally, over the copy machine, a teacher or other volunteer will tell me she runs, to which I always respond enthusiastically and like it is the best and most interesting news I have heard all week. One in particular told me she likes to run, and that her husband runs marathons. I gave her my standard response to the topic: If you can run three miles, you can run a marathon. They always blush and shoo the thought away, but I tell them everything I can cram into a five-minute coaching session, including making the time for the long runs and looking up training plans. Oooh, I love a newbie.

Audrey and I were picking out new everyday athletic shoes for her, and while in line, I overheard a mother talking to her daughter about her being able to run in her new running shoes next time she heads out with her mom. Unable to resist chiming in, I carried on about how I was her age when I started running and that it is a lifelong sport, and how wonderful it will be to share it with her mother. I can almost imagine the pictures of her and her mom finishing a Mother's Day 5K together. Runners beget more runners.

Chapter 11
Entertainment on the Course

I love how races have become not only kid-friendly, but they are also blatantly encouraging young ones to get involved in the sport. Most races, from the small town 5K to the big city marathons, have kid's races and fun runs. They generously distribute the gateway drugs of cheering crowds, T-shirts, and medals—can anyone resist the allure of free food and bling? "Mommy, is this Gatorade really free?!"

"Yes, my love, all this can be yours for a very reasonable registration fee and some laps around the block to prepare. Wanna go pick out some new running shoes, hmmm?" Soon, another innocent child will fall prey to the tangled web of muddy laces and safety-pinned bibs.

The expos are tremendous fun for small people who wait all year to go trick-or-treating and hunting for Easter eggs, because it's a very similar event. They walk around and collect stuff. The expo in Chicago may have been the best one for kids that we have been to so far. A car company had a ball-throwing game, where they won T-shirts and wristbands. Other companies gave samples of juice, frozen yogurt, and granola bars. The kids were handed colorful markers to make signs for their runners, and they even got to write messages on big walls. "We can color ON the wall??" They collected cowbell noisemakers and inflatable tubes to clap together. Audrey has a poster of the city hanging in her room. I think they left that expo with more stuff than I did.

We purchased a sign of the times at the 2014 New York City Marathon expo, stem-less wine glasses with the race logo! Are you kidding me? I was looking for a cool coffee mug, and these little beauties caught my eye. I pointed and said, "I have to have a few of those!" Wine glasses at a running expo. I never thought I'd see the day. Sadly, I have yet to find race logo oven mitts.

The races themselves even have family entertainment as part of the event. At the Space Coast Marathon, they had bounce houses set up, and huge astronaut suits to take pictures in. The Bolt Run in Tampa really went all out with rock climbing walls, bounce houses, games to win prizes, and the kid's run itself. The race's start and finish area was outside the arena, where the Tampa Bay Lightning hockey team plays, so the location alone was a huge draw for kids. That was the easiest race to get my kids to do, simply because of the hockey team factor.

Whatever it takes to get them involved is fine with me. Now, if we could just figure out a way to have child-care at some of these races, women could hop into a few more.

Moms have to come up with a lot of the entertainment for our own private daily long runs, such as the eternal days of things like spring break. Who is it a break for? Not for me. Summer vacation means only one thing: time for moms everywhere to reluctantly disembark from the Freedom Train and get back on duty twenty-four hours a day.

After spending a weekend in Orlando enjoying the over-stimulation of park attractions, we spent our first Monday of spring break at home, waking up to rain, and lots of it. That was fine because we needed a down-time kind of day, and I had just the plan in mind. "Let's make tie-dyes!" I cheerfully suggested.

"Yay!! I know just which colors I want to use. Can we get iron-ons too?" my little artists asked me.

"One thing at a time. Go brush your teeth, get dressed, and grab an umbrella," I directed.

Our wet shoes squeaked through the large fluorescent-lit craft store, and we found the tie-dye aisle, noticing on the way that art supplies were on sale. I thought, "I'll pick some up on the way out," since the kids love to paint. After a few minutes of color considerations, we had our dyes and shirts in the basket and headed over to the art supplies. I was investigating packages of glitter glue when I heard a "Swish, swish, spewww."

"I know that was my people!" I barked from two aisles over. Sure enough, the kids were playing with bouncy balls and foam swords, and smashed open a bag of beads that were rolling everywhere.

"Ugghh, what happened?" Yes, the dumbest question ever. They both of course said it was the fault of the other.

I said, "I don't want to hear it. Ethan, come here and help me pick up these beads." A man working there, who had a slight resemblance to Beetlejuice, approached with the giant janitor mop and said how he wished they would stop selling the swords. Little did he know, it wasn't the swords' fault. A kid looking for fun will find trouble with a cotton ball.

I apologized for the mess and added, "Don't worry, we're stopping at the pet-store after this to get cages." That made him laugh, and he was a good sport about the whole thing. He thanked me for helping clean up the beads, which was nice, but he had no idea the spectrum of things I've cleaned from public floors in the name of looking for entertainment. He also surprised me by saying that most parents run and hide from their messes, which was not cool at all. *We have to teach our young ones not to leave their power gel wrappers in their neighbor's lawns.*

In public, we sometimes see kids, and their moms, at their

worst. It's their most tired, most bored, or even most wound-up, but despite the limping people at the finish line, we shouldn't be scared off. The race is tough, but it's mostly fun. Still, spring break, let's get this over with.

Before they started school, I always loved having play dates at our house, and kids running through playing hide and seek. I enjoyed coming up with cute little lunches, and hanging out with other moms. As they have gotten a little older, it is getting tricky, because this generation spends all summer at organized camps. Kids today have a camp for everything: cooking, archery, all the sports, and I even saw an advertisement for a farm camp, which I actually think Ethan would love because anytime we go to a farm for a festival, he asks me if we can bring home a goat. But when we were kids, we all went from one friend's house to another's, like a pack of coyotes traveling their route and looking for better snacks. I finally started getting them into more camps last year, because they want to be with other kids more and their nerdy mom less. Summer then ends up being a lot of taxi driving and calendar planning, instead of leisure days playing in the pool.

The good thing about a little more structure during the summer, is less time for television. "Audrey, how many times have you seen this episode of *Jessie?*"

"I don't know, I like it," she mumbles.

"Okay, let's get out of the house." The television shows change a little with each passing year. It seems like yesterday Audrey memorized every word of every episode of *The Little Einsteins*. She owned the large, talking, red rocket ship and carried it with her everywhere, and even slept with it. We willingly brought her pal on trips requiring air travel. He's broken in parts, and no longer talks because she gave him a car wash while Daddy was washing the big car, but I just can't let it go yet.

They have progressed to the teeny-bopper shows on Disney.

I am okay with most of them, but I keep a close ear, and sit with them sometimes to see if I have to explain anything. So far so good. These shows are moving at a reasonable pace I can keep up with.

When we go to the movies, it's always for kids' movies. I think only once or twice a year do David and I make it to a movie without the kids, and it always seems weird without them. I like most of the kids' movies, and we have absorbed the Despicable Me Minions and their culture as part of our own. Every day, one of us will quote those movies. David even won a giant stuffed Minion at a basketball carnival game during our most recent spring break.

We had launched this spring break week at the Universal Studios Theme Parks. Going to these worlds of everything artificial is like a race, because it takes a lot of planning, endurance, patience, and you want to carry as little as possible. For us, it usually ends up being a good experience, because rather than trying to do everything in one day, we keep the pace on the slower side, and take breaks after a few long lines or crowded shops. One particular day was especially memorable because the lines were very short, the weather was perfect, and we were all in a good mood, which in itself is a major accomplishment. Toward the end of the day, with only a few more rides to check out, we decided to give The Mummy ride a try. I don't want to ruin it for you if you have never been on it, but I will say this; I am aware of the things that make Audrey fearful, and had I known what that ride included, I would not have suggested that we try it. After we all exited the ride and ambled off the platform into the gift shop, she was still quite shaken by the experience. Ethan, however, loved it, and he wanted to go on again. It took a few hours for her to process what she went through, and as the shock began to wear off, she proclaimed, "That ride was awesome!"

For me, that was an illustration of how I go through life

trying to protect them from as much as I can, but going into something without fear persuading us to hold back, allows us and our kids to see that most things are not as difficult or as scary as we thought. I hesitate to try new things or make new commitments, but it may be time to remove some of the bubble wrap, face some fears, and say "yes" to new opportunities more often.

The rest of the year is of course not spent at theme parks, but often at home where they find ways to entertain themselves. Once I'm smart enough to tell them to turn off the television and the iPads, they come up with some things that entertain even me. Breathlessly, Ethan will skip over to me and say, "Mommy, can I have a shoe box, some string, plastic spoons, and Christmas lights?"

"Hmm, let's see what we can find. What do you need these things for, bud?"

"I'm working on a project."

"Okay, let me know if you need help."

There are scraps of cardboard on his floor, things assembled with too much tape, and cap-less markers surrounding him. "Wow, it looks great buddy!"

"Thanks, Mommy. It's a house for these guys," he explains, picking up three small stuffed animals and giving me a tour of the property. "I'll be right back. I have to find blankets for them."

Shortly after their imaginative crafts, they will both come hunting for snacks, and head outside to run around and ride bikes. Ethan will do about twenty cartwheels in a row until he actually appears like a wheel. He asks me to arm wrestle and go for walks. If we have water balloons, Ethan will be busy for hours. Audrey will invite me to join her in some sidewalk chalk or a basketball game. I am glad that the simple things are still more fun than any of the fancier toys they just had to have from Santa.

I love the entertainment of the kids' school plays and musical concerts. The pre-school and kindergarten years are the funniest, because there is always one who hams it up for as much attention as possible, and always one who just stands there staring off into space, scratching his belly with his shirt up, and not singing even one word. Seeing my kids up there with their few lines of stardom always melts me, and it gives me a chance to see them through the eyes of others. No casual observer would think that a sweet girl like Audrey would intentionally destroy her brother's Wii game. Or that humble Ethan would steal money, candy, and toys from around the house. They all shine in their uniqueness, and we get the swag bag full of warm fuzzies.

I am easily entertained along my running route. I am perfectly content looking around at what nature cooks up, and saying hello to other runners and walkers. Mostly, I just love that I don't need to be entertained while I'm out on a run, because the whole point is to not have to give, or get, attention for a while, and I escape. One of the most common questions I get from non-runners after revealing that I don't wear music on my runs is, "What do you think about all that time?"

That is a long answer. That first half-mile is like the air-lock compartment of a space ship. It is a small space to make the transition from busy mom/student/accountant or your own fill-in-the-blank, to a free runner. The volume of noise in my head gets steadily lower. Once my equilibrium is established, I start smiling, and breathing rhythmically, because with each footfall I can shed the piles of laundry, sticky lunch boxes, and family drama. I can zone out and be numb for a while, and then, refreshed, I can attempt to organize my life for the last couple of miles.

I think we can all agree, grocery lists sit at the top of our internal conversation on the road. While it can be difficult to please everyone all of the time, I love to think about what I plan to cook and eat. I try to start a run already having looked at some recipes, and then finishing the list on the run. Smaller matters such as, "What should I send to my friend for her birthday? Remember to pick up that book Audrey needs for her report. What am I wearing to the meeting?" also take up some headroom on the road.

I spend a lot of time thinking about my kids and how they are doing in school, whether they are making good friends, and when we might have time for the extra activities. But the bigger stuff starts to take a turn, things like, "How can we get her to stop biting her nails? Is he a good enough reader for his age? Despite my short-comings, do they know how much they are loved?"

I also think about the goofy moments of our day, and how sometimes I feel like I'm going crazy trying to reason with tiny people. One minute, I will correct Audrey for back-talking only to turn around to see Ethan taking a bite out of a stick of butter, thinking it's a cheese stick. I can't help but crack up. One minute, you're going uphill, but soon you're on an easy downhill.

Sometimes I think about absolutely nothing and just stay in the zone. Empty. This is when even leaves blowing around might surprise me because I'm just spaced out. It's a relief to be void of all noise or internal chatter, and ring out the dirty water from my brain. Just...Be...Quiet.

A lot of my mileage is with prayer. Poor God, He has enough to do without all my nonsense. "Thank you for the thoughtful prayer, Sheila, but if you saw the morning news, you understand I'm rather busy today." I know a lot of my prayers are trivial compared to others, but He listens to the small just as intently as the ominous.

I thank Him that I am out there in the first place; that my body can do this anytime I want. We can never take that for granted. I pray for the safety and protection of my family, my friends, our schools, everything. I pray for my family members to hear God's call on their lives and know the peace that He can give. I thank Him for the food on my table and the roof over my head. Running can be a bit of a luxury if you think about it, and for each step I get to take, I am grateful.

But during a race, even though there is a lot to look at and entertain our minds, it's hard to take it all in when you are literally running through it. The Gasparilla Half Marathon route has a large section of out and back, so at some point, all us midpackers will get to see the race leaders and elites like a rush of wind, toward the finish. I try to let out a "Woooo!" or clap a little. It never gets old to me to watch a runner go that fast. I wonder what it would feel like to run a five-minute mile. Would my legs literally fall off like beat up tires on an old pick-up truck? Would the speed cause streaks of fire behind me? Would my joints crumble like stale cookies? I'll likely never know, but I like to watch those first runners flying along effortlessly like art in motion.

Chapter 12
But Mommy, I was Here First

My biggest running competition at this age is with myself. The young, elite racing women don't have to worry about me breathing down their necks out on a course. I just like to try to run faster, and be an "age-grouper" at small races. I try to do the best I can with what I've got, so the time goal I set for myself is based on my training, physical readiness, and race day variables. My overall running goal is to enjoy it and be able to do it for as many years as possible.

During a race, I might keep an eye on someone I'd like to keep up with, not necessarily to place ahead of her, but because having someone slightly ahead of me will help me mentally push myself a little harder. Sometimes I do want to catch one and get ahead, but there are times that, no matter how hard I try, I can't reel her in because she surges away with more strength than I have. During a half-marathon several years ago, a woman pushing a triple-wide—yes, triple jogging stroller—zoomed past me like I was standing still. I kept thinking I could catch back up with her. Ha! Not even a chance. I need some electrolytes to wash down those morsels of humility.

I placed second in my age group at two small races, and a

first place in master's division. I admit it does feel undeniably good to earn a medal that not every finisher gets. A few extra chips in the already delicious cookie. The first of which was the summer after the stress fracture and continued healing of the plantar fasciitis. We were on a little Fourth of July getaway and the hotel hosted an Independence Day 5-K. I didn't think much of it since I hadn't been running very much at that point, just still taking my time and cross-training. But, to my appreciative surprise, David registered me for the race scheduled for the next morning. A humid, sunny morning under the merciful shade of the oak trees dripping with Spanish moss in northern Florida was the backdrop to the start line of my first race post-injury. It was a field of only a few hundred runners. The course looped around a golf course and through hilly residential areas. After I finished, I quickly found some ice for my heel, and then blissfully made my way back to the hotel, to find David and the kids at the pool. I was on top of the world and grateful to see some normalcy on its way back to my running.

A few weeks later, I received a letter in the mail from the race organizers, congratulating me on placing second in my age group, which was only about ten, but I was thrilled anyway. I had no idea, since I didn't stick around for the post-race awards. They enclosed my medal which I proudly displayed.

My next age group second place was at the Bolt Run, also a small field, about fifteen to twenty in my age group. I had moved up an age group since the Independence Day 5-K. This was special because the kids were there to see me receive the medal. Audrey wanted to wear it because it had the Tampa Bay Lightning symbol on it, which was fine with me. She looked cute and I'm happy to share.

My master's first place was at a Clearwater Beach ten-miler on a day with sideways winds. I was scraping sand out of the corners of my eyes and ears for days. The kids ooh'ed and ahh'ed over the trophy. This was new, this whole older age-group thing. It certainly was strange to be separated into a whole new category, but it was also a silver lining to be able to still compete with my peers. We all sure still feel very young, even though we were born in the 1900's.

All half and full marathon finishers receive a medal at the finish line, whether tenth place or ten thousandth place. Because they know we love the medals, some races try to lure runners with new and fancier bling, and encourage participants to register for multiple races to get multiple shiny new medals. An anniversary race is always a big deal for the medal designs and we can't help but sign up.

Much controversy surrounds the practice of giving young children medals or trophies for sports for simply being part of the team. The major concern being that it sends the message that making everyone a winner to preserve their feelings will give them unrealistic expectations later. I personally think, for younger kids who may have put themselves out there to try a new sport for the very first time, it's a great thing. Sometimes people fight harder when they are discouraged, but they always want to do better when they are encouraged—a few pats on the back can really help build a person's confidence. So, while they are little and getting to know what they are good at, let them experience reward for effort. It's a great feeling, and as they grow older and find their niche in life, they will understand what it means to work to earn rewards. Ethan has some medals and a trophy from flag football, and I know he takes a lot of pride in those and knows he did his best, even though it's not likely he'll pursue football since it's not his thing. But at eight years old, he can run a 4:02 half-mile. I love that.

I talked both Audrey and Ethan into running their school one-mile fun run with me when they were newly nine and seven. The promise of a shirt and medal in a comfortable envi-ronment with all their friends was an easy sell. Audrey can run —she has a stride without even thinking about it. Ethan can also run, but sometimes goes out too fast and occasionally flings his feet out to the sides, but he's all heart. We can work on keeping those legs straighter later on down the road.

I was nothing less than shocked at how well they both did. I hung back with Ethan while Audrey floated on ahead. He needed a few walking breaks but finished his mile respectably. With spirits high, we decided to pay the fee and hop in the half-mile run. I told the kids, "Okay, you clearly can do this, so every man for himself, see you at the finish." Only a few minutes later, as I was waiting to see Audrey come around the corner to the finish, I saw Ethan, chest forward, arms chugging, boney knees absorbing the impact at full speed. As I cheered his name, I looked around for Audrey, feeling bad that I missed her finish, but alas, Audrey had not finished yet. It was Ethan's race, by two minutes. I was so happy for him because as the younger brother of a confident older sister, he sometimes gets the short end of the wishbone. But that day, he was the prevailing champ of the family, and I found that incredibly fun to watch. Dealing with Audrey after a defeat is always agonizing. She went through her list of reasons why she was so far behind him. That's okay, you tell yourself what you need to, but the racecourse doesn't lie, and your little brother finally got a win.

These two are always in competition at home, even when it goes unspoken. In fact, their competitions are blatantly passive aggressive. After homework, the back door opens so they can escape to their yard and gain freedom from homework. On the way, Audrey will look out of the corner of her eye to be sure she blocks Ethan from passing through the door before her. This starts the epic adventure of "Who Got on the Monkey Bars First" kicked off by piercing screams of injustice.

Pausing from unpacking mysterious things from their lunch boxes, I walk outside for the first of many visits. "Audrey, Ethan, if you fight, you'll have to come in and do time-outs."

"But she kicked me!"

"Audrey, why are you kicking him?" I know I'm not supposed to ask that question, but I am a slow learner.

"Because!! He cut in front of me!"

"You two need to work this out. Take turns and be fair. The next time I hear a scream, you are both coming in. The neighbors do not want to listen to this nonsense."

"Fiiine!"

Only minutes later, the screaming once again stabs my eardrums like barbeque skewers, and I have to force them to come in the house and go to time out. When will they learn that if they operate as a team they will get more of what they want? If they would only remember that if they get along, I might say something like, "Wow, you two played together so well this afternoon, maybe we'll go to that frozen yogurt place after dinner." If they started competing for who has the cleaner room, or picks up the most dishes after dinner, then that would be something to boast about.

I am in the process of scheming to make that happen with these housekeeping newbies. I discovered that if I ask out loud, "Who wants a little job?" They will both say, "Me! Me!"

"Okay, Audrey, do you think you can handle the vacuum?"

"Yes, yes, I can!!"

"But I want to do the vacuum!" protests Ethan.

"You can do it next time. I have another job for you. Audrey, do you remember how to do it?"

"Yes, Mommy, I don't need any help," she says as she's already unwrapping the cord and about to show the family room carpet who's boss.

"What can I do Mommy?" asks Ethan.

"You can take this duster and chase away all the dust from the shelves and tables."

"Yaaaay!!"

I may have discovered a major secret: that by playing to their desire to be better than the other kid in every area of life, I can get some help around the house. I wonder how long this smoke and mirrors effect will last. I'm afraid that at some point one of them will figure it out and I'll have to take back some of my jobs.

Of course, letting my young ones attempt to help around the house means I have to teach them a few basic things I take for granted, such as how to empty the dust from the vacuum canister without creating another mess entirely all over the kitchen floor. Even though they are invited to do what they consider the more grown-up, and therefore more important jobs, they won't be able to complete them exactly as I would, but one step at a time. Consistency will give birth to progress.

Occasionally, Ethan drives Audrey crazy with his irritating little brother antics and sounds. He will do somersaults right near a detailed display of Legos or army men, and she will raise the volume of her voice to blood curdling hysteria. Thinking I have a clue, I remove Ethan from her highness's presence, and take him to another room to play games or do artwork. I was smart to remove the irritant from the room, thereby giving her a peaceful kingdom again. Unfortunately, I have made the grave mistake of giving her an opportunity to think I love him more than her. I can't win.

While I play another round of Go Fish with Ethan, Audrey wants to join in, which will soon lead into another argument over who gets to go first. If at the start of this mini war, I had invited Audrey to go play cards with me, with certainty she would have said, "No thanks, I'm busy with my ducks." There should be no question as to why mothers sometimes look like they are walking through life with electric currents racing up their spines.

Surprisingly, we came across a mother who fed the already burning embers of irrational competition in her children. The kids and I spent a Saturday morning at one of our favorite parks and went to a quick lunch where we spotted a sign for an Easter

Egg Hunt. It was a fundraiser for a local organization, open to anyone, and asked for a nominal donation. We decided to give it a try. It was being held at a nearby recreation building and outdoor fields, and was packed with families. Kids carried baskets and had their pictures taken with the Easter Bunny himself. There were even bunny footprints through the entryway. We enjoyed the crafts, a few games, and even snow-cones. Finally, the hunt was about to begin, so I gave them each a reusable grocery bag since this was an unplanned hunt and I didn't just happen to have Easter Baskets rolling around the back of the car. About a hundred kids waited patiently to begin, and I overheard a mother command her son, "Get right toward the middle as fast as you can! No Mercy!"

I raised my eyebrows, turned to look at her, and said with a half-joking smile, "Wow. Sounds like pretty fierce competition here today."

She immediately started back pedaling because she realized what she must have sounded like, and stammered, "Well, you know, all the kids will start collecting the closest ones first. I just want him to have a good strategy."

"Oh, good point," I agreed, allowing her to save a little face.

But sure enough, it was indeed a vicious fight ring out there. Ethan came toward me saying, "Two! Only two eggs!" He then told me how a girl jumped on another guy's back, tackling him to the ground. The kids were all whacking each other, and some stole eggs out of other kids' baskets. This seemed like the equivalent of tripping another runner midrace. Not cool.

I saw at least three kids walk away crying because they were unable to retrieve even one egg in their basket. It really was a tough crowd. No mercy was in fact shown that day. Don't worry my little man, there will be other races for you, and we'll probably skip this particular one next year.

Chapter 13
Glycogen Depletion and Hitting The Wall

It's 5:00 p.m., also known as: The Witching Hour. Or, *The Wall*. It doesn't matter if we've been home only five minutes or all day, but I can count on a lot of drama at this hour. Your kids may help each other quietly with their homework and clean each other's rooms, but for some reason, mine can fight about anything.

One typical car ride home from school left me spent.

"Hey! Stop throwing that at me!" Ethan asserted his value as a human being.

"I'm putting my stuff in the car, *Priscilla!*" Audrey clarified for him.

"Stop!!" Ethan screeched in a much higher octave.

"What? What am I doing, baby?"

My turn. "Okaaaaaay! Give it a rest you two, or you'll start your afternoon in time-out."

"See, every time it whines, we get in trouble."

"Audrey, stop! Don't start your afternoon like this," I reminded her as my heart rate went up and the heat in my face radiated. "Maybe you should do some more after school activities if you can't get along."

Sheila Scott

"Yeah, right!"

"That's it. As soon as we get home, go to your room. I'll set the timer for ten minutes. If you talk again, I'll bring it up to fifteen." The only reply from her was a silent arm cross and menacing eyes.

Back talk is particularly exhausting because, as they age, their quick wits sharpen, and I can't always keep up. Mentally tackling these hills wears me out, and by the time I replenish my fluids and they are calm and sweet once again, a hairpin turn approaches and we're back in the combat zone. I really need to work on my strategy for those steep and surprising sections of a race.

A few times a year, our school has an early dismissal so the teachers have time for additional training, which is a great idea, and I appreciate their efforts to always be their best, however, when I have to pick them up three hours earlier than normal, I wonder why they can't keep them three hours longer the next day. It's only fair.

During the school year, I try to keep in mind that some days, or weeks, can be especially draining for them too, and they need a little more rest. I can tell if the week of homework was an Ironman, activities were running into each other, allergies were unbearable, and maybe even some kid was meaner than usual. When I remember to slow down my pace for them, it helps us all, and they are soon restored to their effervescent selves. I might allow extra screen time, which can be sufficiently vegetative, or even skip a planned activity to let them rest their parts and hearts.

As the end of the school year approaches, e-mails come in tidal waves, announcing play performances, class picnics, award parties, and of course the need for parent volunteers. Please, stop! My free time is ticking down, and the last thing I want to do is live at school with only a few short weeks of freedom remaining. I of course go to everything and help at everything, and smile happily, even if begrudgingly because in the end I don't want to miss out on these sweet and quickly passing days of their childhood.

Plus, the kids' academics and homework are a lot more demanding than when I was their age. I certainly didn't have book reports and homework in first grade. So even though they look like bottomless pits of energy, rather than racing out the door every day of the summer, I want them to enjoy that down-time and some cut-back weeks, to rebuild their strength. But, keeping them from flipping out over who gets the last blue yogurt tube, depletes my energy stores more rapidly than any race ever has.

The best way to effectively manage the school vacation glycogen stores is to prepare ahead of time. We carb-load for a race, like we activity-load for summer. A few months before school lets out, I begin to make a list on our whiteboard that includes ideas for day trips, crafts, and play-dates. I make a list of all the area parks, especially ones we haven't been to yet, as well as all our favorites. If I am able to give them some struc-tured outings, their free unstructured time is less miserable. They are happy to escape into the adventurous world of their imaginations. The strategy here is to deplete their glycogen at just the right moment so they fall asleep at a reasonable hour. If they hit the wall too soon, I spend the rest of the evening trying to keep them away from each other, calm hysterical fits of crying because "She took my stickers!!" and soothing overtired little bodies to a restful state of mind.

At the close of a typical day, when Ethan was a mere few weeks old, it was getting close to bedtime, the end of a long run so to speak. I knew there was only about an hour left and I was sure I could make it. On this particular night, Ethan was in that stage of crying for two hours between five and seven, and unfortunately for me, David was out of town as he normally is when there is a live creature problem at home. I was walking around the house, trying to comfort Ethan with shaking and jiggling, and soft renditions of soothing Sarah McLachlan tunes while he had his cry time. Audrey was on the floor playing with toys, and she said, "Mommy, look, there's ants here."

"Honey, there can't be ants on the carpet. Maybe it's Gold-fish crumbs."

"Mommy, look." She pointed.

I turned on a brighter light and said, "Ohhhh nooo. Okay, you go to the chair over there. I'll put Ethan down and deal with the ants." To this day, I don't know what kind of ants they were, but there was a good chance they were fire ants.

Those miserable little critters creep up on their victim's foot, and once a jillion of them are assembled, they all bite at once, leaving a person screaming and begging for mercy. Once the ants are removed from the person, small little pimples develop and they burn! *I had to take swift and severe action to eliminate these guys.*

Ethan, now not being held of course, went from normal night-time crying to full blown, red-faced screaming. I ran around and collected Raid and Windex, because Windex messes up their trails and confuses them, and went on an ant killing rampage. Once satisfied that the enemy was defeated, I washed up any poison from my hands and searched the rest of the house, particularly the kids' bedrooms for any more of these things. After finding no more ants, I continued the bedtime routine, starting with trying to get Ethan to calm down from his frenzy. This sidetrack then made everything take a little long and go a little later. Unexpected surprises like that challenged my endurance after I've already put in my miles on the Mommy Mill during overnight feedings, and have been up since 5:30 a.m., the other witching hour. It's also possible that the only other grown up I interacted with was the cashier at the grocery store. Now fire ants? No course detours please! I was making the final surge into the chute!

Oddly enough, sometimes it feels exhilarating to be depleted. A good, long run with a steady pace, no aches and plenty of water, leaves me the very happy kind of tired. Yes, I want to lay flat and elevate my legs, but I'm blissfully worn and oddly cleansed in a way. I feel good about my efforts, and grateful for completing a successful long run.

That happens for me as a mom sometimes too, the days where I get it just right. I love the warm feeling at the end of the day, after the kids are in bed and the house is quiet, and I reflect on how we spent our last fourteen hours, knowing it was a good run. I still had all the same household tasks, played hide-and-seek with them, maybe went to the park, set-up and took down the slip-n-slide, took them for haircuts, fed them consistently, and read a pile of books at bedtime. The route was pretty much the same, but I was calm, peaceful, able to handle their skirmishes quietly, and even with a dose of inspiration. So, as I absently watch another episode of Chopped, I also feel privately proud that they went to sleep happy and peaceful, feeling good about themselves and about our family. It's a happy tired.

Other days it's a hopeless, dismal kind of tired, when I think I should let the kids run the show and go lay down in the fetal position by myself. Like an ugly run with cement shoes leaving me groggy and grumpy, maybe even feeling not good enough. My patience is depleted, I'm frazzled, and forgetting—or unable —to slow down the pace. 5:00 pm is just as much my witching hour as it is theirs. If I let my energy get too low, or heaven forbid, eat too much sugar on an empty stomach, primitively thinking I'll perk back up—Beware! That is a lethal combination where likely even a slight misstep will cause me to wreak havoc. "Whoever left the milk out will now suffer my wrath and face eternal doom!! Rooarrrrr!!"

It took me a long time to notice the pattern of how sugar on an empty stomach affects my state of mind, but once the light bulb went on, I knew enough to reach for rice cakes with hummus instead of yesterday's brownies, and my glycogen-depleted temper tantrums started decreasing.

True depletion happens at the deli counter. At our grocery store, the meat they sell is from a company that requires strict and specific handling of all the products to ensure food safety. Fine. Love that. But mysteriously, it does not matter if there are eight people ahead of me or only one—it takes the same amount of time: *Forever.*

While we wait, Audrey will likely put her hands somewhere on the cart and ask if she can push. To which I reply, "Probably not," relying on memories of past trips when I let her push. Ethan meanwhile is taking more tickets from the Please Take a Number machine as Audrey nonchalantly pushes the cart directly into him.

"Oowww!!" he screams. Sigh, here it comes.

"What? What did *I* do?" This is her standard response to start mind games with me. But I'm so naive, I think I can reason with a nine-year-old and tell her what she did, forgetting that she in fact knows exactly what she did and is internally cracking up at getting away with a mean jab.

"Cut it out, you two. The better you behave, the quicker we can be done." Has this line worked for anyone yet?

"Mommy, can we get toaster pastries?"

"No way, those are dessert, not breakfast."

"Awwwww," they harmonize.

Ethan asks politely, "Mommy, can you take me to the bathroom?" Of course he has to go now, because my number is next.

The bathroom thing is a moving target. When we go to dinner as a family, David thinks it's silly for me to take them to the bathroom shortly after ordering, because he'll correctly remember, "They manage to ride bikes and swing for hours before they need to come in to use the restroom." But my experiences help me to know for a fact that the very second my plate is lowered to the table in front of me, one will ask to go, so I try to plan ahead.

"Ethan, can you wait a few more minutes?"

"No. I need to go nowww."

"Audrey, will you take him?"

She does love a position of authority. "Okay! Let's go Ethan!" The stomp of the flip-flops echoes through the store, and I can hear them on their route. They return promptly and not fighting as I yell, "Bingo!" when they call my number.

"What can I get for you today?"

"Hello. I'd like a half-pound..."

"Mommy. Mommy. Mommy," Audrey predictably interrupts.

"Stop, I need to order our things."

"Sorry, I'd like a half-pound of roasted turkey breast..."

"But Mom-Meee!!"

I plug my ears, smile and add, "Sliced thinly, please."

"Mommy!"

"What Audrey??"

"Never mind."

"Oh, for crying out loud, you finally have my attention, and *now* you're going to be quiet?"

I say thank you to the woman at the deli and press on. We've only just begun this adventure. Like a mud-run, I know there are obstacles ahead. Audrey will casually kick Ethan while I am choosing tomatoes. Ethan will draw smiley faces on the condensation-filled windows of the freezer department, and they will beg for candy with admirable fervor and tenacity. I am spent, empty. As soon as we get home, I will suggest they play outside for a while so I can reboot.

During a race, we all feel our energy wane at some point. The 5:00 p.m. of the marathon, better known as The Wall. We appease it with energy gels, raisins, a good song, encouraging mantra, or prayer. Whatever it takes to trick ourselves into believing we can get these last few miles behind us quickly. Whatever you do, stay calm. Getting upset will waste too much energy and deplete you even faster. The same way you can never let the kids see you panic because that's when they know it's time to pounce! It is no longer a physical race to accomplish miles or daily tasks—it's a battle of wits.

The most difficult finish to date was in New York 2014. Oh, it's great during that last couple of miles into the finish, exactly what you dream it would be, and then once across the final timing mats, they toss you a medal, a shiny metal blanket, and a bag of snacks to get you through what I have dubbed, "The Zombie Parade."

I haven't checked a bag at a race, other than one time simply because it's kind of a pain. In New York, if you opted out of checking a bag, they promised you a poncho with the race logo. Fine by me. I'd take another souvenir and have David meet me with a sweatshirt and a cab ride. *Not so fast sister.* The bag-less runners were guided to one side of the walkway with the repeated and enthusiastic promise that "You're almost there!" *You keep saying that, but we're still walking on a path that seems to get narrower every few feet.* If you wanted to sit down for even a short rest, no can do, nowhere to sit. You had to stay in the zombie parade with no clear end point. If it weren't so cold I'd have taken my shoes off because my feet were killing me. I wanted to untie those laces and give my toes some freedom. But we kept on marching.

Thirty minutes later, we made our way to a main road and were lovingly wrapped in our ponchos by volunteers who I am certain had halos over their heads. These ponchos went to our mid-calves and were like the ones the NFL players wear on the sidelines, basically a blanket with a hood and sturdy Velcro closures.

The zombie parade was well worth the awesome poncho, but once again, I was not done. Hoping to meet David and the kids at FAO Schwarz, I tried to cross at Columbus Circle, but because of road blocks for safety of the race, I was re-routed backwards and around a few buildings until I could cross over. I asked a man who was waiting behind the ropes for his runner if I could use his phone to call my husband to let him know I was running a bit late. He was happy to help me out.

Fighting the winds and the crowds of spectators, but wrapped in my poncho of luxury, I kept moving, limping up and down curbs so I could get to the comfort of my family, and a warm store. No matter what comes a mom's way, she has the mental toughness for endurance, even when the race is over.

After a long stretch of training and racing, runners are encouraged to enjoy a period of rest from running, to replenish energy stores and let muscles recover. After a marathon, I avoid running for about at least a week, and even then, it's just a few miles, and very gently done. It may have been a bit more after Chicago. I imagine little cartoon bandages running around, taping up micro tears and checking blood pressure. This week of rest, of course, is merely a rest from running, not from the responsibilities of life. It's also a chance to finish reading that book I started months ago, clean out the garage, and have lunch with some friends. The recovery after depletion is for our parts *and* our hearts.

Sheila Scott

The very same people who look at me in disbelief when they ask how much I ran on any given day, are the same ones who come up to me and ask, "Are you training for any races right now?" A non-runner isn't aware of our cycles of running. It's very thoughtful for them to ask, but when I'm feeling worn out from a long stretch of training, I just say that I'm taking a break for a while and doing some cross-training. I am not a spring chicken, and I take the recovery phase seriously in hopes that I won't miss another race because of an overuse injury, and more importantly that I can still be running a few good miles when I'm eighty.

But I don't think we ever get a complete recovery from the trials of motherhood. We have to wear our bib number every single day. Even if I try to take it off and go incognito to the bookstore with a coffee in my hand, someone will likely call me out. "Hi! Aren't you Audrey's mom?" Darn it, I was found.

Audrey is a talker, for which I am grateful because she tells me what she sees happening around her at school, how she is feeling, and asks me questions about every topic, including the ones that I am not ready for. Ethan is also fairly chatty so he'll jump in on her comments with his own point of view, and soon they are cracking up about some kid at school who got sent to the office because, in front of his whole class, he responded to the teacher with an emphatic "Whatever!" when she explained that night's homework. They often make me laugh out loud, bringing me some needed energy.

But week after week of childhood drama, visiting-the-deli-kind-of-moments, listening to Minecraft updates in excruciating detail, the favorite color of each of the band members of One Direction, and that within five minutes of going to play on the monkey bars I will hear Ethan crying about something, I speed right past tired into despair. I feel like a sponge, soaked and dripping, unable to take on more water. I need to ring out the old water before I can absorb any more energy or give any more attention.

When I am a few miles past worn-out, my mood sinks, and I am at greatest risk for saying something I will likely regret. But even if one of these children did something way out of line, every once in a while, I realize I can dole out undeserved grace at the moment I most want to hide in my closet. Wouldn't it be great if moms got sent to time out? Imagine being stuck in your room with only books and zero technology.

Choosing to ask Audrey if she wants to play a game of Around the World at the basketball hoop in the driveway or joining in their wrestling, automatically stops the downward spiral from spinning out of control. It is a tiny miracle that lifts all our spirits and restores us back to somewhat normal people. Soon, we will laugh, hug, and feel good about each other. This technique works with running every single time I think I can't move a muscle. No matter what life drains out from me, if I can get out there for even thirty minutes I come back with multiplied energy. Running, like kids, can simultaneously deplete and revive us.

After several weeks of a busy travel season, David was on a golf weekend with his friends. I know, I know, it seems silly going on a golf trip if you live in Florida, capital of golf, but he works hard and needs a break just as much as anyone, so I try to be a good sport, knowing that he'll come back refreshed, travel will lighten up, and he'll be around more. I came down with a pretty bad cold, not debilitating, but unpleasant, with a drippy nose and a sore throat. I would have loved some time to veg out, but of course, like all moms, I pressed on as though nothing was wrong, and faced the entire weekend alone with the kids. We kept busy with homework, teacher appreciation cards, piano, and playing outside. Naturally there was plenty of arguing and back talk sprinkled throughout the weekend to add to the challenge of keeping things together.

When David came back, he asked how I was, and at that point I was a lot better, but that the worst day was Saturday. I told him I was completely congested all day, walked around in a fog, and popped throat lozenges one after another. Not to mention, I was just plain tired, the kind of tired that puts weight on your shoulders. You will not in a million years guess what he asked me next. I promise, I am not making this up, ladies. He innocently asked, "Did you rest?"

Pause. I have to decide if I calmly merit this question with an answer or flip out. Hmmm, what would you do? Okay, I flipped out.

"Are you serious?" I lowered my voice. "*Seriously?*"

I imagine he realized his horrifying miscalculation at this point, still fishing golf tees out of his pockets. "Yup, I took a eucalyptus aroma bath and sipped chamomile tea while I watched my favorite old movies on the couch, it was an extremely relaxing weekend." The benefits package for moms does not typically include sick days.

I almost felt bad for him at this point, that silly man. I pick on him, but he is a great dad, always at the ready for fun with the kids, and when he shifts out of work mode, he's *really* out of it and totally focused on the kids.

And once I feel better, I'll arrange a dinner out with my friends, or have a random few hours when he takes them ice skating or fishing. Not everyone can be on a break at the same time, but moms can push through until we reach the next aid station.

Chapter 14
Post-Race Party

Runners are friendly but subdued before a race. Some quietly stretch and do high-knees. Others mill about wiggling out their arms, or sit to the side pressing the lumps out of their socks. Those that aren't subdued find it very important to tell every single person the long list of races they have completed in the past year and every injury ever suffered. I love outgoing personalities, but that can be rough when you're trying to get in the zone. Moving closer to the start line, it gets chattier, but conservatively so as the runners await the gun signaling them to go ahead and begin their next milestone. Some are out there desperately seeking a PR, some are in their first race ever, some are adding a race to their long streak list, and some are after the ever increasingly difficult Boston Qualifying time.

No matter the purpose, the end result is a crowd of heavily breathing, red-faced comrades who are now bonding while comparing notes from the race. They talk of calf muscles seizing up, or how trying a new energy bar was a mistake, and who outran who in the last few yards. Whether a long race or a short one, a lot of preparation goes into getting to the start line, and for making it to the finish. At that point, the celebrations begin. Everyone savors that wonderful feeling of personal accomplishment, along with the fresh bagels and live band.

Post-race celebrations are such a big deal to runners because there is always, no matter how slim, a chance that a runner might not finish. When I signed up for my first marathon, I read a lot of race-weekend information, including the part about runners being required to finish in seven hours, because after that time the course would be closed. Seven hours is a long time, and I have been a runner most of my life, but I couldn't help pause and wonder, "Holy cow, what if I don't finish before making it to the banana tent? What if a medic vehicle has to come find me and bring me to the lost and found? That would be embarrassing." Again, not a likely scenario, but I wonder if most first-time marathoners, and 5K'ers don't feel that same knee-jerk flash of irrational fear.

Finishing a race is not simply crossing the last of the timing mats under a huge clock surrounded by flags. After the clock in Chicago, I stumbled to the sweet volunteers in dry clothes with no sign of crispy salt in their eyebrows, and gratefully accepted my medal. Then, I wrapped myself in the comforting shiny metal blanket, and a few steps later I was offered bags of ice to which my quads answered, "Yes, please!!" I found a quiet spot to the side of the chute and sat with other finishers and their strategically located bags of ice.

Once rested, I limped my way past the snack table and accepted my box of goodies, grabbed a water bottle, and finally glided out of the chute all together. One more step and I was back into the real world—that part of the party was over.

David and the kids never did get to see me during that race because by the time they got to the points where they planned to look for me, I had already passed. But before the race we chose a meeting spot, knowing the finish would be busy and tight with security. I asked for directions to our agreed location and learned that it was quite a distance in the opposite direction of our hotel, so I asked to borrow the phone from a woman at a race tent and left a message for David to meet me at the room instead of wandering around.

I gingerly made the lengthy walk back to the hotel and found them at the indoor pool, splashing around having a ball. I chose to go back to the room and get the stink off. Our poor washing machine would probably be in tears when this little outfit made its way there the next day. Once home, David actually used the garden hose on my running shoes and left them outside. I wasn't insulted, *I knew.*

The next part of the party was limping around the city on a sunny evening, clean, and proudly in my race-logo jacket, hearing my medal clanking into my dinner plate, and nodding to the others doing the same. I was happy to be out and about among the other race-logo-clad limpers.

After Audrey was born, we were on top of the world, and that celebration kept going for longer than we expected. Sure, lots of cards, flowers, and gifts showed up the first weeks after her birth, but it was at eight months when the last of the "new baby" gifts showed up. Eight months! I wrote more thank you notes that year than after our wedding. It just goes to show, however you become a mom, it is regarded as such a big deal and such a singular experience that people just can't help but celebrate.

Motherhood is the one endurance event with no finish line. Or worse, a mirage of a finish line, that as soon as you think you are close, it moves further ahead. The race-director announces on the bull-horn, "Hold it right there, ma'am. Just 'cause you figured out age six, doesn't mean you can handle age eight. Keep going, follow the arrows, and keep the cones on your left." But since I love making it to the finish, and to parties, I keep chasing this ever-moving line of accomplishment.

Two years after the 2010 Disney Marathon, Ginny went

back to the motherhood start line, excitedly welcoming her second baby daughter onto her team. I vicariously joined the route to story time, play areas, and splash parks. I saw her carry the diaper bag, overstuffed with puffy rice snacks, chew toys, and extra clothes. It was fascinating to watch it play out all over again, and every time I see her small daughter I can't believe mine were ever that little. It feels like a lifetime ago.

Along the way in life and running, we get milestones and celebrations to reward us for the leg of the race we made it through. Many people say that the first year of raising a child is the hardest, although I am refraining from deciding which year is the hardest, since I am gratefully oblivious as to what is to come. But for conversation, let's say the first year really is the hardest.

Everything was new, and I really did learn as I went along, as I still do. I was tired from being up during the night and early in the morning, and getting through each day of feeding, changing, and chasing. At Audrey's first birthday, I got that invisible pat on the back that said, "See, you did it. The police didn't have to come look for you and find you lying in the fetal position in the diaper aisle. Great job. Now try year two." Audrey had a "Fun to Be One" T-shirt that she wore a lot that year. It would have been nice for me to get a race shirt too, something that said, "I Survived My Baby's First Year, What Day Is It?" The sponsor list on the back of the shirt would be formula, diaper, sippy-cup, and coffee companies.

Audrey's first birthday, and Ethan's too, were very small, with just our little family, and my parents came to stay with us. I also had a little playgroup shin-dig during non-napping hours, with a handful of friends, but that was it. It was plenty for us because instead of focusing on a big, grand party with clowns and ponies to clean up after, we really got to look at our one-year-old miracles and savor them, along with the greasy frosting that coated their hair.

Since then, the parties have ranged from being big ones at the house with forty kids running around, to gatherings at the infamous bounce house places, complete with penicillin in the goody bags. One year, Audrey asked if instead of a party with her friends, if our family-foursome could go to a water park in Orlando and stay overnight in a hotel. David and I loved that idea, and it was one of the most fun weekends we have spent together. I thought it was so cool of her to pick that kind of celebration for her nine-year mile marker. Ethan too chose an "event birthday" one year that involved Pooh Bear and friends. It was a celebration not only for them reaching another year—it was a celebration for our family team as we made it through another mile together.

The kids have little victories throughout the year, and always get a post-race party to enjoy. Every aced spelling test, caught fish, and new friend made is a little achievement to be proud of on the way to completing another year of life, or of school. They get hugs, high-fives, and ice cream. A great report card might get a reasonable trip to Target. I said *reasonable*, don't take advantage.

Like my once-a-year marathons, we treat New Year's week in a similar way. It's a lot of fun, but a lot of work, so I'm glad it only comes once a year. Many years ago, before either of the kids were born, our traditions of New Year's began with David's family coming to stay for the week. These days, with the four of us already here, it has grown into having eleven people in the house. Year after year, the planning became more focused to ensure an optimal good time, always shooting for the next PR in holiday hosting. I approach it like choosing a training plan. Spreading out cookbooks to plan menus, making lists of nearby day trips to see some sights, and our collections of extra blankets and pillows has grown to be able to support a small hotel. I stole an idea from a bed and breakfast in Savannah we stayed at shortly after moving to Florida, and I keep a guest book for all of our visitors to record the dates of their visit, and the highlights of their trip. Talk about a funny training-log.

Once our Christmas mayhem passes, we tidy up the house, of course keeping all the decorations and lights up for added festive feelings, and rearrange rooms to accommodate air mattresses and luggage. You can feel the excitement in the air in anticipation of our family's arrival as one of us shuttles back and forth to the airport. The noise levels and camaraderie steadily climb, and shoes are piled up at the entryway. At the table, the family catches up on each other's lives and what kept them so busy all year, while they gobble up the cookies—go ahead, load up, I learned to keep extras in the freezer. The scene is so familiar in some ways, like that of a team at a coach's table, but now, I'm the coach.

Leading the family holiday festivities, the coaching generally starts with it being clear my family has never packed for a race —they forget everything. "Sheila, can I have a nail clipper, a swimsuit of David's, and a pair of pliers?" David's older brother will ask me.

"What in the world do you need pliers for? Never mind, I don't want to know. Here you go."

Just like the kids do, they will ask me what the dinner plans are, and since every family has a few picky eaters, the menu options are very strategic. They will ask the mileage of a loop of my neighborhood, and if the pool is warm enough for swimming. Since it is December, the pool is not even close to warm. But one of them will end up doing a polar plunge anyway. The same way that big races have something for everyone, including those not running, our week is like that too. Some will go golf, some will go shopping or to a movie, but we always end up back at the table.

Truth be told, I didn't always have an appreciation for this week. Imagine hosting this family week with a baby and a two-year-old, and then a two and four-year-old. It was a lot and there was plenty of groaning. My organized and consistent life, now in complete disarray—I don't even want to talk about the condition of the floors. But somewhere along the way, I learned to relax and have fun. Most importantly, to not worry if everything was perfect.

One year, the day before the arrival of the family, I brought Ethan in the house from the car in his little infant carrier, and placed him on the kitchen floor. But, running out of counter space, I smashed my glass cooktop with a bag of canned tomatoes and canned sauce, which were intended to begin making the annual lasagna. Oh boy. How do you cook for eleven people without a cooktop? I went to the corner drugstore and bought a small crock-pot, the hot plate that wasn't allowed in college dorms, and set out the take-out menus. This worked fine because usually a few times during the week, my mother-in-law from Buffalo would say, "Let's just order a pizza." No one cared about the broken-down-stove, they just wanted to laugh over old stories and have fun. Things go wrong in a race, but you slap on some Vaseline from the popsicle sticks at the medical tent and keep going.

One year our septic tank was gurgling, and every time I heard a toilet flush, I listened for someone potentially screaming, "Oh, gross! The toilet is overflowing!" We had the septic guys come as soon as possible, but eleven people were banned from using the bathrooms or running any water for eight hours. We kept going to the mall and fast-food restaurants for potty breaks. It would have been handy to have our own porta-potty that year.

After carb-loading with the heavy lasagna, our highly anticipated round of White Elephant Gift Exchange gets underway— some of us have been planning our gift for months and await howls of laughter as it gets unwrapped. Between gifts, we have to stop and applaud the washing machine for all its extra miles of towels and sweaty golf clothes. "You can do it! Keep going! Only a few more days!" And that poor recycling bin—he can barely stand up with all the extra weight of the week, I think he pulled a muscle.

We usually have more local friends over, and set up as many tables for Euchre card games as we have people to fill them. Meanwhile, the pack of kids will run outside playing flashlight tag and beg the dads to come out to help them with sparklers. The kids are up too late, and we all dance along to New Year's Rockin' Eve on the television, with goofy crowns on our heads and noisemakers at full blast.

Like a long race, this week requires plenty of endurance, but is a wonderful, although temporary, celebration. It's a break from all the hard work through the year and meant for us to spend time as a family. We strengthen our bonds, away from car-pools, offices, and committees. And before we know it, multiple trips are once again made to the airport, the fridge is cleaned out of all contraband, air mattresses are deflated, and the steam cleaner erases all evidence of a good time. Just like that, we cross the finish line and go back into the real world, ready to start all over again.

In hopes of yet another post-race party, I did a little more research on Boston qualifying standards and decided to give it a go, having the benefit of six previous marathon experiences and a lot of life lessons about consistency, proper fueling, and choosing a destination marathon with the kids' entertainment options in mind. The course on which I would attempt a BQ was Richmond, Virginia. The very long hills were not the reason I chose that course, and despite the grueling training, I was slightly, although blissfully, unaware of how long these hills were really going to be.

I chose Richmond because we have a lot of friends and family in the area, and I knew I could count on much needed spectator support. I told them which mile markers where the sight of their faces and sound of their cheers would be most beneficial. We enjoyed time with our family, had a comfortable hotel just blocks from the start line, and lots of friends to hopefully celebrate with the night after the race was completed.

As ready as I could be with Hal Higdon's Advanced Training Plan, I set off with the 3:45 pace group. I was flying along with them, perfectly comfortable. The weather was sparkly sunshine and comfortable, cool temperatures. Climbing up mile ten, I saw my husband and kids. That was the first of the hills and it was okay, I felt great. The runners in my pack were all chatting away like it was any other day out for a group run. Then mile fifteen came.

We had just finished a very lengthy climb, the kind of climb that makes you think, "Well, I can try to BQ another race. I'll just take it easy." Until your rational self wakes up from its lactate binge and says, "Enough of that kind of talk, and get your legs turning over for crying out loud!"

At the top of this climb, I tried, but as we started crossing the bridge into the city, the wind came at us head-on. I had no choice but to recover a bit and then pick it up later on. I knew if I tried to sprint to catch the pace group, I wouldn't have had any gas in the tank in the later miles. So rather than the race really getting going around mile nineteen as it usually does for me, this internal banter started at mile fifteen, and I would have to keep telling myself to hang on, that I was still in it, and it was all mental at that point.

Still windy, mile nineteen was tough, and we still had two more good climbs ahead of us. One minute I was invincible, the next I just wanted to sit down. It helped that Ginny was in Richmond that weekend visiting her family, so seeing her and her little daughters along the route gave me a much-needed boost for a few miles.

I saw my best friend from high school, who lives in Richmond now, along mile twenty. At that point I was pretty sure if I kept my current pace, I'd be cuddling with my BQ in a little while. I was shouting something about going to "Haavaad Yaaad!" Energy back on.

David and the kids were cheering for me again at mile twenty-four, where I looked at him with a grim expression saying, "I don't know, it's going to be close..." To which he ordered me to pick it up, finish what I came there to do, and then called me by my maiden name. That guy is the king of making me laugh and cry in the same instant.

But he was right. I had to keep trying. With only two miles to go, I had to leave everything on that course with no regrets. My feet were killing. I passed a man at mile twenty-five laying on the street clutching his calves in agony. I felt terrible, and yet we all know that absolutely anything can happen in a race. My calves were still on board so I picked it up, turned the right-hand corner into the downhill stadium-like finish lined with cheering spectators, and knew by the clock I had done it. I earned my BQ. I was going to Haavaad Yaaad!

I saw Bart Yasso at the finish and thanked him for the Yasso 800 workouts and, hunched over, I told him of my achievement. I tried to find the leaders of my pace group to thank them, I was only a few minutes behind them. That pace group was a big help for almost half of the race. People that we barely know are often a big part of our post-race celebration, even if they don't know it.

After a much-deserved sprawl on the grass for a few minutes, I pulled myself up with the help of a kind, nearby tree, accepted my water and pizza, and limped up a flight of stairs leading from the park, back to the city streets. I made it to my hotel, where my sweet kids and hubby were waiting for me. time to celebrate!

I applied for registration for the 2017 Boston Marathon and made the cut off time by just under two minutes to get a bib! This was a miracle of sorts because only a month or so before my goal race to achieve a BQ time, the Boston Athletic Association made the time standards five minutes faster for each age group. Five minutes is actually a lot of time in a marathon, so I had some doubts that I could accomplish this goal.

Being in Boston with my family for that race was an unforgettable and cherished experience. Many of you know what that city is like for race weekend, it's running-nerd heaven. A hard race though, and the downhills are much harder on your body than I had expected. Everyone talks about the uphills, but the pain is in the downhills.

The finishing chute funnels us toward another start line, and sometimes the distance between the two is a little blurry. The kids are sprinting ahead, so, okay, I'll choose to be a little uncomfortable and try to keep pace with them. Maybe these are the downhill days of motherhood. It seems a little easier as they get more independent, and yet it's painful too.

At another school year start line, I fish out the backpacks that have also been on break, and reinstate "the routine." I will likely volunteer to be room mom again—I just can't seem to help myself. I will look for some races to pop into and look forward to my own weekly mileage. I know the course will be filled with tears and fears, back talk and blisters, hurdles and hurts. There will be setbacks and surprises. I will glance at the framed pictures on the walls filled with memories and mile-stones, and will not be afraid of steep hills or trials, knowing that the joy will outweigh them both, and new traditions will be born. We know that after every push beyond our limits, there will be a little celebration, and we will once again experience that warm, magical feeling, although more fleeting with time. These are the Miles of Motherhood - and we're in.

Epilogue - Moving Up an Age Group

I wrote this book in 2015 and continued to dabble with it for a few years following, but it just sat in the laptop as one of those dreams moms sometimes put aside, maybe also because of a teeny bit of fear. We all read the training books for improving times, incorporating strength and optimal nutrition. Many of us have read the inspiring biographies of famous, well accomplished runners. I love the running novels by John L. Parker, Jr. and have read them multiple times. But I wanted us to have a book that celebrated our lives, where we could chat and laugh about our average days and feel connected in our, behind the scenes, but incredibly special, experiences. I hope by sharing some of my stories, you are reminded and warmed by your own.

So, ten years is a big jump in age groups. The course is a lot different and has passed all types of scenery: fun, laughter, love, but also illness, heartbreak, and some unplanned routes. You might look back and wonder how in the world we got through some of those miles.

In races, years also matter. We are grouped by age and gender, typically five-year increments, sometimes ten in smaller races. Despite facing the fact that we're getting older, there are benefits to moving up an age group. If we stay consistent in our running, largely injury free, and remain fairly fit, we can start winning age group awards. The fifty-something crowd starts thinning out and slowing down a little, so it's very rewarding to still race hard, and sometimes get the little plastic trophy at an event. More importantly to me, is the mere fact of still being out there, participating, meeting runners, and focusing more on the health benefits—physical and mental. My goal of achieving epic PRs in races is slowly shifting to racing for the pure joy of lining up at a start line.

Another benefit of moving up an age group for many, is the illusive Boston Qualifying Standard. It's not exactly as simple as hitting the minimum required finishing time in an approved marathon, so I am grateful to have qualified three times and was able to run it twice. A huge life goal and dream come true. Actually, I never even dared to dream that I could do it. I always thought it was out of reach. It wasn't until I surprised myself with a fast race in the 2013 Chicago Marathon that I thought I could have a go at it. After a few attempts, I qualified, and I ran Boston in 2017. Well, shuffled might be the better word. I was severely unprepared for the effects of the downhills on my legs. At mile twenty-two I saw David and the kids, and I thought my ankles were broken. The pain was shocking. It was unlike anything I had felt in a marathon before. I ran again in 2025, very well prepared for the downhills, and ran it over eight minutes faster than in 2017. I was nursing a little calf injury, so I ran conservatively but felt great, and made peace with that race.

The other milestone event in 2025 was Ethan graduating from high school. New age group, new bib, and new start line— Empty Nester. Much like I had a panic attack before my first child was born with the transition, the identity crisis, and the great unknown. Here I am again. *Now* who am I? I have to figure this out *again?* I spent a total of eight years serving as room mom in the kids' pre-k to eighth grade school which certainly became part of my identity, but it's not meant to be a lifetime position. If I'm confessing, I started these volunteer positions as an attempt to continue to use transferable skills, so I would have something to put on a resume if I hopped back into career mode at some point. What I didn't expect was the gift it was to have that amount of time with my kids in those fleeting years. Plus, I got to know all of the kids, the families, the teachers, and staff. It gave me something to be part of, and added sweet memories of the kids growing up.

We navigated east coast hockey travel with Audrey, and high school golf with Ethan. The kids made new friends and earned new freedoms. A few chapters back, I talked about the hardest part of motherhood. Spoiler alert, the hardest year wasn't the first year, not by a long shot. It was when we taught them how to drive. So far, for me, this is the absolute hardest part of parenting. We truly have no control each time they drive away. Not even the comfy *illusion* of control. How can this little kid who fishes in the pond down the street be driving my car? By *himself*? How is this little girl with the duck driving an hour to a hockey rink? They are moving up age groups too.

I also started trying out my increased independence and joined a race committee for our largest annual race weekend in Tampa, called The Gasparilla Distance Classic. It has four different race distances up to a half marathon. Runners come from all over the country, and some internationally, to run. It also has a fantastic race expo, always very big with a lot of vendors and speakers. It takes place in late February, which is a beautiful time of year to be in Florida.

I spent four years on that committee, meeting wonderful people, and learning all sorts of things that happen behind the scenes of races. The number one thing being that the volunteers have a much harder job than the runners on race day. We were mixing sports drinks and unwrapping finisher medals at three in the morning! But the excitement was contagious, and we had a ball those weekends.

In the blink of an eye, high school was wrapped up, and instead of driving to different hockey rinks, we drove around looking at dorm stuff, and cute college clothes. The dining room became the staging area for the packing. Audrey was incredibly excited to start her new life, and when your kid is happy, you are too. Right? Yes, but the ache in my heart just sat there, knowing that there was a shelf life on having lunch together and watching Gilmore Girls.

I cried for a solid month when Audrey went to college. But through the tears, it was fun to see the new rhythm of just me, David, and Ethan taking shape. We figured it out and it was a special time. I was less of a disaster when he left for college two years later, but still had a few weeks of weeping and fighting the weight of the silence around the house. I couldn't believe how quiet it became. We all remember the days when a silent house sounded like an impossible dream, but when it arrives, it's not quite as fun as we imagined. What I wouldn't give to have a few more nights reading to them snuggled in their beds, or going to a park, or even settling landmark cases over who *actually* owns the markers. It all added up to being a couple of unforgettable, crazy, magical decades.

Audrey and I have been a very close mother daughter duo sharing walks, shopping time, lunch after church on Sundays, plus all the time we had together on her hockey trips. Ethan and I also had our own favorite outings over the years, mini-golf, biking, going to the zoo, and kayaking off a local beach. He always paddled a little faster than me, sometimes brought along his fishing pole, and we enjoyed the sea life together in the toasty sunshine. Before he left for college, he kept his promise to go kayaking one day with me, so we picked up shells, swam a little, and walked through the soft, white sand. A day I am grateful for as we capped off the end of his summer.

But empty-nesting is not all just escaping for hours in the scrapbooks I worked so hard on, or hugging one of the hoodies they left behind. Our relationships are changing and growing. Obviously, we will always be their parents, but we are seeing shifts into being buddies and having easy fun together. Visiting them at college is a joy and a surprise each time, because we get to see who they are becoming. I love when they call and I look forward to the visits, but the fact is, it changed. As quick as the finish line tape gets crossed, it all changed. Coming home to an empty house after visiting them at school knocks the wind out of me a little. They are becoming new people, and so are we. All we have to do is decide who *we* want to be next.

And I love learning new things, but anyone that knows me knows that technology is where the love of learning ends. It's just not my thing. Many years ago, David surprised me with a new phone. I actually cried. It completely stressed me out. But I am challenging myself to become more comfortable with tech. I upgraded my running watch recently—well, it was an anniversary gift. I'd much rather have running stuff than jewelry or designer purses. It took me a while to figure out all the fancy things it can do and remember which button leads to which function. This watch can do almost anything. It tracks and analyzes your every inch of forward movement, elevation, VO2 max, and calories burned. It predicts how you could perform in races. It practically bakes a meatloaf!

The learning curve for new empty-nesters and new college students is steep for both groups, and steep hills are tough. But we have navigated new routes and horrible weather on race day many times before, and we can certainly handle this. They are figuring out who they are in a new environment, without us available at every turn. We are figuring out how to let them go, to be needed by them, but in different ways. Like the youth of the Sandhill Cranes, the previous two decades were headed steadily in this direction and we knew it all along. I can't see the road ahead, what jobs they will have after college, or where they will live, but I know we will conquer all those bridges when we get to them.

The images of my own future are a little fuzzy. Still not *really* planning on trying out for the Rockette's, but am happily a member of a community chorus, which is almost the same. Lol. I'm golfing more and many days it's just me and sweet, fluffy Benny, who is also moving up age groups.

I will keep races on the calendar, attend more of my running club group runs and continue to enjoy those sunrise miles. There is a house just past my neighborhood where a man who is probably in the eighty-year-old range runs the perimeter of his property. He's dressed in a cotton T-shirt, knee-high socks, and even a terry cloth headband. He's out there plugging along, happy as a clam. Every time I see him, I hope that will be me when I'm eighty, still cranking out a little mileage. And although the miles are maybe a little fewer, or slower, and even though we have made some wrong turns, our fancy GPS watches will help us get back to the route. Because we are approaching the next Miles of Motherhood, and we are *still* in.

Acknowledgments

Writing a book is often a solitary experience, much like running. I am grateful for the people who were with me to help me get it, finally, over the finish line.

Thank you to Gabrielle Speth, my editor, who has eagle eyes and spot on instincts for things that needed adjusting and sometimes left on the cutting room floor. She was encouraging, yet honest, and helpful with so many little questions along the way. She also created the sweet little doodle on the dedication page. Her talent is limitless and I aim to work with her again soon.

Thank you to Shannon Walsh, my formatter, as I mentioned, technology and I get along only so well, so her skills were among the most important and appreciated.

Thank you so much to my friend Ginny who talked me into running that second marathon which is what planted the idea for this book in my head. She has encouraged me from the very start of this book idea and has been one of my most enthusiastic spectators.

Thank you to my track and cross-country coaches from high school, especially Mr. Williams, for encouraging not only me, but every student on those teams, to believe that we could achieve our running goals.

Thank you most of all to my husband David, for being a husband and friend far beyond anything I ever dreamed. For taking care of the kids or driving them somewhere so I could get a long run started long before the Florida sun came up. For traveling with me and the kids to so many marathons and making them special family trips with thoughtful details. For every card of encouragement and for all the goodies at all the expos. I am most grateful that we were able to make a way for me to spend these years with the kids. I am so thankful for everything you did and love you beyond measure.

Audrey and Ethan: Without you I would not have known the depth of joy motherhood brings. I have loved every single second with you both, holding your tiny little bodies, hearing your laughter and watching you grow. My heart is overflowing with memories from every year of your lives, and I am incredibly proud of the people of character and integrity that you both have become. My prayer is that you work hard for your dreams, stay close to each other and always know how much you are loved.

Lastly, thank you to moms, mom figures, dads, and dad figures, as well as my own mom and dad. Thank you to my mom for driving me and a pack of my cross-country teammates to or from our summer running camp almost four hours away, and for thinking it was cute when I ate spaghetti and toast the mornings of Saturday meets. Thank you to my dad who understood what a special sport running is and for making it to a few meets despite the distance. To you both for still taking an interest in my running over forty years later.

Moms, mom figures, dads and even mentors stand in the gap and help make what might be "the difference" in a child's life. Big or small contributions, it all adds up to a wonderful team. Without the spectators cheering us on and volunteers at the bagel tent, races would be really boring. Thank you for being there.

All names in this book have been changed, however all stories are true from the author.

www.ingramcontent.com/pod-product-compliance
Lightning Source LLC
Chambersburg PA
CBHW070921130626
46555CB00001B/222